DAMN, IT FEELS GOOD
TO BE A BANKER

DAMN, IT FEELS GOOD TO BE A BANKER

And Other Baller Things You Only Get to Say If You Work on Wall Street

BY

LEVERAGED SELL-OUT

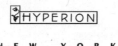

NEW YORK

Copyright © 2008 Leveraged Sell-Out LLC

Library of Congress Cataloging-in-Publication Data is available upon request.

ISBN: 978-1-4013-0968-8

Hyperion books are available for special promotions, premiums,
or corporate training. For details contact Michael Rentas,
Proprietary Markets, Hyperion, 77 West 66th Street, 12th floor, New York,
New York 10023, or call 212-456-0133.

Design by Jo Anne Metsch/JAM Design

FIRST EDITION

10 9 8 7 6 5 4 3 2 1

This book is dedicated to

165 Church St.

—the most prestigious

apartment building, ever

Contents

Contents

Preface

LET ME BEGIN by saying that I'm not writing this book for any of the reasons all those hack junior college creative writing all-stars dream about writing a book.

I'm not writing this book for money; I bonused ten times the advance I got for this my first year out of college. I'm not writing this book to get chicks; I am an Adonis. And, most important, I'm not writing this book for any sort of literary cachet; most writers are pretentious, ill-educated douchebags who couldn't break 650 on the SAT I Math Section. I got 1600 (unrecentered), twice.

I'm writing this book because it needed to be written. I represent a group of individuals whose work buttresses the world's economy, and while I normally wouldn't give a fuck what the proletariat thinks, I figured it was time I set everyone out there straight and explained what Banking is really all about.

Every other book on the industry has been written by a jaded 10th tier loser who wished he were more "creative" or some clueless writer spewing esoteric nonsense. As such, I figured it was time that a real Banker stepped up to educate the world on the important realities of Banking and its lifestyle.

This is the result—a book of Banking facts that will introduce you to an amazing world that you'll never be able to become part of.

Dad, thanks for not letting me study liberal arts.

Logan

Business

FACT #1

No. We do not have any "hot stock tips" for you.

Industry

IN THE FALL OF 2005, I moved to New York City to work as an Analyst at a Bulge Bracket Investment Bank. Leading a wave of other recent Princeton graduates, I casually stepped from one of society's most elitist playgrounds to another. It felt completely natural. Since then, my friends and I have made the city our own. Frequenting The City's hottest night-clubs and bars, we throw the best parties, and we experience its most beautiful women. Essentially, we run shit. We dominate The Scene, and it is all facilitated by one overarching fact: we work in finance.

To clarify, we don't work in the layman's concept of finance (fī'năns), spoken with a long "i"; we work in finn*ance* (fə-năns'), the refined English pronunciation reserved for only the upper echelons of the industry. We are "Bankers," but not in the traditional sense. When most people think "Banker," they're really thinking of Retail Bankers—those who offer loans and credit to fledgling T-shirt stores and overeager franchisees. Retail Bankers wear golf shirts they buy on eBay, live in North Carolina, and get home at 6 p.m. to eat dinner with their kids. As Investment Bankers, we are their polar opposite—we spend thousands on any given night, wear suits the price of automobiles, and work intimately with the world's most high-profile businesses.

That fall, I moved into an apartment in one of TriBeCa's most exclusive areas with seven guys from school. Five guys ended up living in an apartment upstairs, and three of us took a place directly below them. Getting the apartments was a breeze; when our Russian landlord saw the names Goldman Sachs, Morgan Stanley, and Blackstone written all over our applications, his face lit up with delight. "Gold men and sex!" he proclaimed, prophetically. He was so confident we'd be good tenants, he even offered us a "very special rate." Cheap things generally suck, so we doubled it.

Investment Banking

I chose to live in the three-man with the two guys the rest of us didn't know that well, not out of kindness, but because I wanted my apartment to operate efficiently, exactly like an Investment Bank.

Corporate Finance

My room, with floor-to-ceiling windows, southern exposure, and its own private bathroom, is the Corporate Finance arm—the Investment Banking Division (IBD). I help companies raise capital and advise them on mergers and acquisitions. I conduct in-depth, highly quantitative analysis that requires both the utmost intelligence and extreme diligence. Starting out, I often worked upward of one hundred hours a week, pausing only to instruct the world on nightlife best practices and to budget my Bonus. Hearing about this schedule, people often naively asked, "When do you sleep?" To which I offered the only logical response: "If I wanted to sleep, I'd have been a surgeon."

Sales and Trading

My roommate Jon is in Sales & Trading. While IBD is often referred to as the "library," S&T is the "locker room," and from the Gold Bond–ish stink of Jon's room, it's quite obvious how this nomenclature came about.

Sales at a Bank is just like sales anywhere else—pushing stuff that people don't want down their throats. In this situation, however, financial products and trading ideas are being peddled, and since it's an Investment Bank calling, people actually pick up the phone. Jon, a Trader, prices and executes the trades that the sales group has orchestrated. Jon lives and dies by the market, waking up at 6:30 a.m. before it opens and getting home around 6:30 p.m. after it closes; it even dictates his bathroom habits, forcing him to be able to go in less than fifteen seconds so he can return to sit by his obsession, vigilantly. It would ruin the Bank I have created, but I've been not-so-secretly hoping Jon will move out, taking with him his jock straps, empty beer cans, and sweat-wicking Under Armour button-downs.

INSIDER INFO WITH MORGAN, A COMMODITIES TRADER

For the record, Traders aren't freakin' Bankers. Yes, some of us might work at Banks, but I mean, Bankers are SISSIES, bro; Traders are MEN. Don't forget it.

Bankers play with computers and make graphics and shit all day. Fuck that! We bring in actual money for the firm, son!

Shit. Call me a fucking Banker and see what happens. I played rugby in college, man, not some lame shit like squash. You think a Banker could hang with me on the pitch?

By 10 a.m., all a Banker's done is recheck 500 formulas in a spreadsheet; my group's made like $10MM, and we haven't even warmed up yet.

Ask me a math question. Go ahead, ask me! I will do it in my head before you can even blink! Ninety-five times 12 is 1,140, BAM! Automatic, baby, automatic.

Instinct—that's what Trading's all about. Show me a Banker who's got raw instinct, and I'll show you how to open a beer bottle with your ear.

Equity Research

My third roommate is Gopal, who works in either Fixed Income or Equity Research—I always forget which, but they're both a joke. He deals with debt or writes seventh-grade-level reports on stocks, respectively; irrespectively, he's a wannabe. He's the smallest, gangrened, and brownish arm of Investment Banks, and while he's often annoying, he occasionally provides some utility. Just so Gopal's role was clear, we stuck him in a 150-square-foot room with no windows carved off of our living area with a pressurized wall. There is a thin slit at the top of his door, however, which lets in just enough light to remind him how comparatively bleak his life really is.

Consulting

For a few weeks when we moved in, we had a Consultant* crashing on our couch. He worked for a place called Boston Consulting Group and earned a pittance. From what I gather, he toiled away in a conference room for an unimpressive seventy hours a week before delivering PowerPoint "play books" or suggesting a non-English-speaking Indian call center as a means of increasing productivity. Despite the name of his firm, he never worked out of Boston, which might have been somewhat acceptable; instead, he bounced from one Bumblefuck part of Ohio to another every week, coming home only on the occasional Friday night before heading right back out on Sunday. He wasn't quite prestigious enough to

---

*Consultant here means Strategy/Management Consultant. IT consultants, financial consultants, and actuarial consultants would not even be allowed the honor of standing under the awning of our building. They would be around the corner in an eighth-floor apartment of a walk-up building with rats, a crazy Polish superintendent, and no A/C, sweatily clinging to one of those mini-fans you had in elementary school. And the fan's batteries would be dying.

hang with us, though, so we had to boot the Consultant, forcing him to live strictly in Comfort Inns out of his well-worn Tumi suitcase.

In the flood of Princeton students who moved to New York my year, there were maybe one or two graduates who were "testing out finance" before moving on to business school or into different careers. I imagine they are now on welfare. Most of us real Bankers, one and a half years later, have landed even better jobs in finance, and in a few months we'll be moving from the Sell Side (Investment Banking) to the Buy Side (Hedge Funds and Private Equity).

Hedge Funds

Hedge Funds are, in essence, companies that make third-world-country-GDP-size bets on changes in the market. They'll bet on stocks, bonds, the green tea market, the amount of fluctuation in the green tea market, and, for sport, the number of peasant workers who will die for that fluctuation in the tea market—virtually anything you can attach a price to. Hedge Funds exist as individual entities or as proprietary desks trading a Bank's own money, and they employ a wide range of strategies (Macro, Value-based, Event-driven, Special Situations, and so on). But while they might be betting, Hedge Fund guys aren't "gamblers." They're "arbitrageurs."

Hedge Funds are 100 percent driven by results and compensate and fire their employees along these same lines. As such, successful hedger guys are generally performance-driven individuals: ex-Traders, poker stars, and Fantasy Football Hall of Famers. Also, as a result of these stringent metrics, unsuccessful hedgers quickly become unemployed, alcoholic stay-at-home dads.

Private Equity

Hedge Funds are a lucrative business, but I'm personally moving into Private Equity (PE), which carries even more prestige. Only a select few are able to land these jobs, and it's the end-all and be-all in finance—the coveted inner circle of truly badass Bankers. If I even whisper the term *PE* around people I can see them visibly shiver. We're the real Financial Executives, taking pools of money gathered from institutions and wealthy individuals to invest in nonpublic companies (or public companies we take private) to grow, turn around their business, or sell off pieces of them for a profit.

Before I knew all the details of the Buy Side, a female friend of mine from school, Whitney, started dating a Hedge Fund portfolio manager twenty years older than she was. He did all the things a proper boyfriend should do: flew in her friends from around the world, sponsored their chauffeured shopping sprees, and made a production of paying for everyone when we all went out to dinner.

Meeting him for the first time, I introduced myself and told him my name.

"Oh, I know," he responded casually, shaking my hand. And with a confidence glowing almost brighter than mine, he patted his monogrammed cuff. He further explained his omniscience: "I work on the *Buy* Side," he said, as if the emphasis would clear everything up.

I paused to consider this statement. *Wtf does that mean?* I thought. If I had told him the name of my tailor, would he have already known? Had I said: "Your girlfriend cheats on you religiously," would I have gotten the same response? At the time, it wasn't entirely clear why he should have had seemingly in-depth information about everyone and everything. "I work on the *Buy* Side" seemed insufficient to explain infinite knowledge. But now, after getting a job at one of the most prestigious PE shops, I use the phrase all the time.

FACT #2

I smell synergy.
Hierarchy

'VE NEVER BEEN a fan of the whole concept of using the Internet to get girls; it lacks a certain level of finesse, especially when compared to getting a table at a club and just letting them walk over to me. Plus, at work, my computer is the tool with which I build and shape the economic landscape, and call me old-fashioned but there's something not that sexy about a girl who knows how to use my hammer. Wait, I take that back.

My roommate Gopal, on the other hand, might never meet a girl if it weren't for technology. It's how he meets 90 percent of the four girls he hooks up with, and he even has this weird ritual where he will bring his laptop into our living room, connect it to the TV, and project his Facebook account onto the fifty-inch screen.

"Virtual Game Time!" he screams excitedly, as if we should all come running. Occasionally, my Trader roommate, Jon, and I will emerge from our respective rooms, plop down on the couch, and humor Gopal's little hobby for a short while.

The "game" is Gopal's application of finance concepts and terminology to getting girls via Facebook. He also refers to it as the FBAX—the Facebook Ass Exchange. It's a concept he may not have originated but has certainly refined.

It all started when he created his profile a year or so back. He was late to Facebook, but fell in love with it immediately and obsessed over his "**IPO**," Initial Public Offering.

In Banking, when a company IPOs, it is raising capital and putting itself up on the public market. An Investment Bank **underwrites** this process—it helps the company find investors and then structures and trades the financed funds. A large part of the effort in this process is the **pitch book**, a massive document that gives detailed financial and qualitative information about the company in question as well as the Investment Bank's history.

For weeks before Gopal actually IPO'd, he asked us to help underwrite him—Jon and I both had established Facebook accounts and could have helped Gopal in his search for cultural capital. He would have to issue some **debt** and directly request friends, but we could have let him post on our walls or orchestrated some other virtual **roadshow** to draw **equity** investors to him.

As underwriters, Investment Banks generally earn not only fees, but also profit from keeping pre-IPO shares of the company for themselves and selling out after an initial market "pop." But in Gopal's case, there was no such incentive.

During this early period, if Gopal was anywhere remotely interesting or if he thought his hair was looking particularly awesome, he would stop and make someone take a picture of him. "Just working on my pitch book," he'd say casually, as if he were creating a graph of a company's five-year EBITDA projections.

Gopal started out small, adding about 7 people his first week public. He's been steadily trending upward and is now a mid-sized stock with a **market cap** of about 220 friends. The other day he called us in for some FBAX trading, and we reluctantly sat on the couch as the main page loaded.

I felt like I was in front of a massive **Bloomberg terminal**. Just like at work, I had access to detailed information, news feeds, and status updates; Gopal had even color-coded his keyboard for added authenticity.

His main page showed one new friend request. When advising on **mergers and acquisitions (M&A)**, Banks will do **accretion/dilution analysis** to spot synergies or negative effects that might result from a transaction. For example, eBay did this poorly when acquiring Skype; it hasn't helped them at all. We weren't about to make the same blunder.

The request was from a relatively unattractive girl. We knew, however, that **markets** are crucial, and we delved in a bit deeper to see whether she had access to any worthwhile groups or was connected to any networks of good-looking females. She wasn't.

"Ignore!" Jon and I shouted in unison, and Gopal obediently rejected her.

"Wait," I said, having spotted a detail in the friend request. "It said that you two were related?"

We learned that the girl was actually Gopal's first cousin, but, like a good Banker, he stood by his analysis. "Whatever," he justified. "Can't be destroying value like that."

True.

The computer went somewhat haywire for a second, and a series of ads popped up. One of them was for a sale at Neiman Marcus, and Gopal got all excited, talking about how he needed to go pick up some new clothes. I realized his **beta**—a measure of how correlated behavior is to the market—was very high. Betas generally run from 0 (uncorrelated) up, and since Gopal reacts even more strongly than the average consumer, I put him at around a 2.1.

I got up to grab a drink while he closed the dozens of windows and realized that my beta is −1; I react completely inversely. "Ugh," I thought, pounding some Fiji. "Who wants to wait in those lines?"

When I returned, Gopal and Jon were conducting some **due diligence** on three girls to potentially add to Gopal's portfolio. In Banking, due diligence is done before anything. All the available information must be gathered and analyzed before any decisions are made.

The three girls were:

These girls' profiles might have been "bitch books," but since they were already public, they were essentially their **10-Ks**—the statements public companies issue to report performance. Just as a 10-K offers financial information and

Name:	**Jackie**
Networks:	Harvard Alum '06
Relationship Status:	Single
Looking for:	Random Play
Hometown:	Blank, Illinois
Interests:	Golf, wine, Sex and the City, partying it up in Montauk, The Hills, shakin it, surfing, pole dancing at S Factor, and of course Leonardo DiCaprio movies!

Total Friends: 913
P/E Ratio: 85

Name:	**Shilpa**
Networks:	Stanford '06
Relationship Status:	Single
Looking for:	Dating
Hometown:	Newport Beach, California
Interests:	Love Actually, tennis, squash, surfing, all sports really, traveling, Radiohead, reading in Bryant Park, playing lots of games

Total Friends: 220
P/E Ratio: 20

Name:	**Lindsay**
Networks:	Washington University in St. Louis '05
Relationship Status:	It's complicated
Looking for:	Friendship
Hometown:	Lower Merion, Pennsylvania
Interests:	Dinosaurs and unicorns. If you made me pick: dinosaurs. Red licorice, anything organic, anything Lethem, swiping the free cherries at Trader Joe's, wordplay.

Total Friends: 8
P/E Ratio: 3

can tell an investor whether a company is manipulating earnings, overpaying its CEO, or being audited, we were able to conduct **fundamental analysis** on these girls' profiles to come up with reasonable **valuations**.

1. On the surface, Jackie seemed like a great target for Gopal to try to hook up with. She was a good-looking, single Harvard graduate looking for "random play." But our keen financial senses told us otherwise.

A common statistic considered for companies is their **price/earnings (P/E) ratio**; it tells how much each share of the company costs relative to income. With online profiles, more photos generally allow you to assess a girl more accurately. The caveat is that many people strictly post "money shots," which highlight only their best qualities. To offset this, Gopal considers his own P/E ratio, which he has defined as photos/exposures, where *photos* is the total number of pictures available for a girl and *exposures* signifies the number of distinct angles and poses in these pictures. (Do we see lower body? Are there any front-on pictures or are they all profile? Is there a swimsuit picture? Etc.) Like a real P/E ratio, his isn't perfect, but it can be used for guidance.

Jackie had a P/E ratio of 85—she had a lot of photos online from several different angles. Her body was tight; she seemed like the kind of girl who, at the sign of even a few bips (1/100th of a percent) of weight gain, would quickly deny herself her only meal, a midday Pinkberry. The photos ranged from risqué to flat-out skanky. With her rather high 913 friends, our assumption was that this girl must be inundated with messages from random, sketchy guys. Gopal was tracking her relationship status for a couple weeks, and it had been extremely **volatile**.

Jackie was perhaps a solid near-term opportunity for an

aggressive, good-looking guy, but that isn't Gopal. He had to employ a more **value-based** Facebook strategy, and we concluded that she was overvalued and not worth his time.

"I'm **short** this bitch!" Jon screamed, obviously more into this process than I was. We moved on.

2. Shilpa appeared to be a great all-around pick, perhaps even a long-term hold for Gopal. She had an average number of friends and enough distinct photos to indicate that she wasn't cloaking any weird features. Gopal opened up Microsoft Excel, and we saw he had done a significant amount of **modeling** on Shilpa's scenario. Bankers often look at **comparable companies analysis** to gauge the value of a company based on other, similar companies. In his spreadsheet, Gopal had fifteen comps.

We paused to reflect on how pathetic a loser he was, but the comps were encouraging, and he decided to **get long** and message her. It wasn't a pure **hedge**, but Jon suggested that Gopal reduce his risk exposure by poking several of the "comparable cuties."

3. The last girl we considered was Lindsay, and she was a speculative play. As a target, I liked her. She was cute but possessed a latent hotness that hadn't been realized. There weren't enough pictures to be certain, so she carried an inherent risk. She only had eight friends, and we discovered her boyfriend was just some loser who worked at Urban Outfitters. I thought Gopal should "take her private," fix her up a bit with some makeup and clothes, and then go back public with her.

This girl piqued the PE guy in me, and I let out an excited: "**LBO** Opp!"

PE firms often make their money via **leveraged buyouts (LBOs)**. These are situations where the PE firm has spotted an undervalued company that it can buy, reengineer, and sell for a profit. We didn't need **leverage** (to borrow money), but this was exactly what we decided to do to little Lindsay.

Gopal started strategizing on his exact approach, and while the FBAX was fun for a moment, I had officially grown bored of the exercise. I briefly considered a couple of the financial concepts Gopal didn't have in his game. There were no sense of **cash flow**, no **liabilities**, and, more important, no **EBITDA**, arguably the most telling aspect of a company.

I left the living room and got back to doing less geeky activities. From down the hall, I heard Gopal devising a new "ass flow" metric, then shook my head as he burst out laughing in self-amusement.

Overwhelmed by his lameness, I walked back to where Gopal was seated, paused, and slapped him swifty across the face. Then, as he held his hand to his swollen cheek and looked back up at me remorsefully, I could tell he understood: behaving like a real Banker does more for your game than any stupid Web site.

FACT #3

Have it on my chair
by morning.
Terminology

WHEN I ENTERED BANKING, the rigid hierarchy I had heard about was indeed in full effect.

In most groups, there are about twenty or so Analysts, around ten Associates, several Vice Presidents (VPs), and a few Directors and Managing Directors (MDs). From these buckets, smaller "deal teams" are built for individual work streams. This ladder is given a Mafia-esque respect, and orders propagate downward, unquestioned.

Analysts

Analysts are the foot soldiers, actually staying up all night, banging out the spreadsheets and PowerPoint presentations that are the cornerstones of the world's financial markets.

We're the top 1 percent of the top .05 percent of the ninety-ninth percentile of the under-twenty-five population, and instead of playing pool in the back of some Italian deli, we're seated together in a cube farm known as "the bullpen," getting well over six figures a year direct-deposited into our bank accounts.

Early on, there was an Analyst in my group, Andy, a real "gunner." We both performed well, but I, a "hitter," did things casually and instinctively, while Andy backstabbed and brown-nosed like an overly competitive go-getting little bitch. What kind of schoolyard name is that anyway, Andy? In true gunner fashion, he was the kind of guy who had little mirrors set up on his monitor so that he could see whenever our MD came around and prepare to fawn appropriately. To be fair, the mirrors had some utility, but I despised looking over at Andy's monitor, which was always cluttered and filled with despicable #N/As from incorrectly implemented Excel functions.

One day, Andy was bragging about some cheap $70 shirt he had just bought at Charles Tyrwhitt, and our MD walked by and accidentally spilled a cup of coffee on him. Of course, when it happened the gunner didn't say a word, he just dabbed his burn wounds with a soiled napkin and told the MD: "Oh, this old thing? No big deal."

But the rest of the day, Andy complained to his other gunner friend about how his shirt was ruined. I guess those mirrors must not have been aligned right, because our MD came by and caught him mid-whine. The gunner turned bright red and shut up instantaneously. Our MD stormed away but came back five minutes later and slapped $300 cash on Andy's desk.

"Go get yourself a new fucking shirt," he said, matter-of-factly. Andy sat motionless, frazzled.

"But give me that one on your back. Because I just bought it."

And he made the gunner work the rest of the day in his undershirt.

Associates

Associates are technically one rung above Analysts, but in general, they're less intelligent and worse off. While Analysts have the flexibility of moving onto the Buy Side after a couple years, Associates have pretty much missed their shot. They come in many hideous breeds.

1. The post-MBAs who are taking on their first job in finance. Clueless and disoriented, they speak in a messy jargon that they use to pad their limited knowledge.

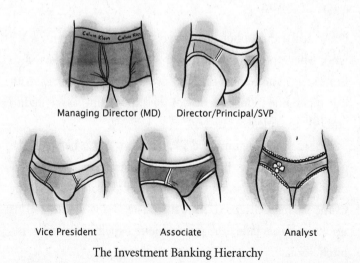

Managing Director (MD)   Director/Principal/SVP

Vice President   Associate   Analyst

The Investment Banking Hierarchy

They easily fall into fits of frenzy that are followed by weeks of depression in which they question their entire lives.

2. Analysts who "stuck it out" for three years and decided to "stay with the firm." Translation: "I couldn't get a job in PE." These are battered wives without battered wife syndrome—they hate their husbands and want to leave them; they just can't find anyone better to house them.

3. My Associate. Very good at nothing. A disastrous combination of the above two types: he worked in finance, went to B-school, couldn't get a Buy Side job, lied about it, and then came back—a battered wife with a worthless degree.

Vice Presidents

On a deal I did about a year ago, I was working with a VP who, when speaking to his Analysts, consistently referred to himself as "The Game." I'm not sure whether he came up with this nickname independently of the rapper, but he seemed to embody the title even better.

He was the consummate VP, stuck in limbo between the junior and senior Bankers. "The Game isn't execution-oriented," he'd insist, with an Ebonics flair to his tone. "The Game is *client*-oriented." But then The Game would call us up ten minutes later, screaming about a spelling mistake in a pitch book.

At thirty-two years old, he still went out to clubs with us to throw money at girls ten years younger than him—a laudable effort, of course, but still kind of depressing. Twenty-five-year-olds on the Buy Side made more than The Game, but after so long in Investment Banking, he was doomed to a life of Sell Sidedness and could do nothing more than try as hard as possible to inch himself up a couple more rungs. He was a nice guy, but to me, it seemed that The Game was pretty much over.

(Managing) Directors

The position immediately above Vice President is referred to by a variety of names: Director, principal, Executive Director, or Senior Vice President. Occasionally, it's skipped and the VPs that make it jump straight to Managing Director, MD. While ordinary Directors might not "manage" enough to earn the extra *M* of prestige, they still "manage" to make a couple million bucks a year.

In the grand scheme of finance, Directors and MDs are generally not as celebrated or well-paid as Hedge Fund Managers or Partners with their own Private Equity shops, but within Investment Banking, they run the show.

They are the ones responsible for bringing in and maintaining relationships with clients. They go to the opera, to lavish banquets, and to gallery openings—anywhere they can cultivate prospective business opportunities. Once the business is brought into the Bank, they are essentially out of the picture until it's time to present the work, at which point they put back on the charm and make sure the "sit-down" (the deal celebration dinner) goes well.

In every Banking group, there are a couple International Analysts. Through some pairing of foreign charm, exaggerated ignorance of American culture, and parental networks, these Analysts are able to completely disregard the Banking Hierarchy.

It may not come up for a couple months, but eventually it's revealed that the International Analysts working beside you are sons of luxury hotel moguls from England or daughters of Kashmiri saffron barons. After university, they spend a couple years in the United States to polish themselves with some Banking pedigree before they return to "the family business." They use this term because it sounds modest, but within Banking, everyone knows what it means. It's not a meager dry cleaner's or corner store they're referring to; "the family business" is a multi-billion-dollar steel conglomerate.

Their parents' companies represent huge opportunities for Banks, and as such, International Analysts receive immunity— they can be drunk, boisterous, and irreverent without any fear of repercussion. We had one such Analyst in my group— Sebastian, from Argentina.

He was both intelligent and hard-working, but he wore ostentatious clothes and came to meetings minutes late, somehow getting away with it by blaming time-zone differences. On one particular occasion, our deal team was out at a bar for a celebration, and Sebastian was rowdily encouraging everyone to do shots of some spicy, aromatic liqueur. Almost everyone complied, including a thirty-four-year-old mother-of-two VP.

Our MD, generally a reserved, polished senior Banker, re-sisted, but Sebastian didn't relent. In his oblivious way, Sebas-tian, seated right next to the MD, pounded shot after shot. He preached the various merits of Fernet-Branca to him, insist-ing that even though we hadn't yet eaten, it would help di-gestion.

Our MD tried to get up and escape, but Sebastian fol-lowed, continuing his sermon. He just kept on talking, using his hands liberally for added emphasis. Finally, after about an hour, either Fernet ran out of curative qualities, or the Argen-tine just got totally hammered. At that point, now drunk and staggering, Sebastian pointed his finger at the man five rungs and two zeroes beyond him in the Banking Hierarchy, slammed his hand down on the bar, and in his thick, lilting accent screamed: "FUCK YOU!"

The professional chatter in the bar immediately turned to silence, and a young Banker Chick fifty feet away shrieked, as if a homeless person had just walked in. But our MD, calm and reserved as ever, just stared back at Sebastian. After a moment of looking into the eyes of insolence, he took the glass in his hand, lifted his chin slightly, and tossed the shot back. The movement was elegant but casual and practiced, such that a tinge of ex–frat boy shone through.

None of us ever knew whether it was Sebastian's disarming

accent or the fact that his father was high up in the Telefónica Group, but after our MD slammed the shot glass on the bar, he leaned back, laughing, and slapped Sebastian lightheartedly on the shoulder. "Stomach's feeling better already!" he announced. Then he ordered another round for everyone.

INSIDER INFO WITH LAUREN, A SYCOPHANALYST

My MD is my hero. He's like the dad I always wished I had.

My MD made MD when he was like twenty-seven or twenty-eight or something nuts. I'm not sure exactly when it was, but it was the fastest ever.

My MD brings in more money for The Firm than anyone else.

My MD once threw a book at and nearly killed this guy who complained about being worked too hard.

My MD pointed his finger at me one time and called me "his resource." I nearly fainted.

FACT #4

Your firm sucks.

Institutions

ONE'S TAXONOMIC AND hierarchical placement as a Banker is important, but the size and esteem of the institution one works for is even more crucial. This final piece of prestige is what separates the real hitters from everyone else—pitchers and catchers.

I have four friends from school with whom I go out to dinner regularly. We'll meet up on a Thursday or before a big Saturday night, stuff ourselves, and get rocked. When the check comes, we don't split the bill; instead, like Bankers, we credit-card-roulette it. The waitress will have already been engaged by our wit and confident advances, and she'll happily oblige when we ask her to take off her hat or panties and toss in our cards.

We instruct her to pull them out one by one, dramatically, and to charge the last card with the entire massive tab.

Bulge Bracket

Out first is my Amex Black Card. Anodized titanium, it's stealthy and sleek. The waitress blushes and it's obvious she realizes the magnitude of what she's just touched. I have to pry the card from her hands as she bats her eyes at me, and it appears as if she might just jump on top of me right there, pantyless.

I work at a Bulge-Bracket Bank, so I'm used to this kind of reaction. Bulge Brackets are IPOing the next big media company, we're advising the merger of the two largest consumer products companies in the world, and we'll even take a moment away from the cool shit to facilitate the building of hospitals and low-income housing so that the world is a better place. Respect.

We're the kids who turned down the Rhodes[*] and Marshall[†] scholarships because the companies we now work at have even stronger brand names. In the league tables, which track Bank deal performance much like a bathroom wall,

[*] Me.
[†] Ibid.

we're ahead. We're the "cool kid" lunch table where if you sit with us, everyone knows, and if you don't, you'll do anything to gain acceptance.

*Notable Institutions: MGM—Morgan Stanley, Goldman Sachs, Merrill Lynch**

Commercial/Investment

Regaining consciousness, the waitress reaches in and pulls out an Amex Gold Card. She recognizes the mini centurion, but it's obvious she loves him less. She hands it back casually to my friend Taylor.

Taylor works at a "Money Center," a commercial Bank that acquired an Investment Banking arm to round out its portfolio. He's a good guy, and his firm is one of the better ones in this group. But as with our cards, a keen observer can spot many differences between us.

Primarily, Taylor lacks a certain added edge of confidence that comes along with knowing you work at the *best* place. His clothes hang on his body instead of floating, as they do on mine. He walks with an almost-strut, but the cadence occasionally loses rhythm.

I don't mind Taylor's flaws, but the very concept of his Bank troubles me. Merging Commercial and Investment Banking feels to me as if they've decided to keep a construction worker and a forklift guy in the same room as an architect who's

* The Blackstone Group's Investment Banking arm receives special consideration among the Bulge Brackets because of spillover private equity prestige.

trying to design a fully solar-powered building. It's like taking a Porsche and attaching a huge MAXIMA decal to the back windshield—it's disgusting and wrong.

Taylor also happens to be somewhat short and, like the Bank he works at, has a Napoleon complex. They both can't get action based on their looks alone, and they "throw around their balance sheet" to compensate. The deals his Bank and those similar to it work on get them a few points in the league tables, but their business is about as bland as the cum laude kids who work there.*

Notable Institutions: JPMorgan Chase, Citigroup, HSBC, Bank of America, Wachovia

Middle Market

I don't even know Jeff. Someone else brought him along, and I hate him for it. When his MasterCard comes out and the hologram and cheap yellow and red logo reflect in the light, the waitress scrunches up her nose and kind of just flicks it back at him, disgusted.

Jeff works at a Middle-Market Bank, and oddly, he's very proud of it. He talks about his work with the gravity of a cardiologist describing a quadruple bypass, but his Bank has done only two deals of note. They mirror his two female conquests, recounted and elaborated upon with transparent attempts at new twists.

* Summa in da house!

Notable Institutions: Dresner, Piper Jaffray, Jefferies, Houlihan Lokey

Boutique

Marlo's card is the last to get pulled out, and he's the one who has to pay. None of the rest of us would have cared about taking down the bill, but when Marlo realizes he's lost at yet another thing in life, the hurt is written all over his face.

The waitress pulls out his flimsy WaMu Check Card and she immediately bursts into laughter. We all hang our heads in embarrassment.

"*I* don't even have one of these!" she jeers, pointing at Marlo. She calls over her waitress friends to come look, and they all inspect the card like it's the silliest thing they've ever seen.

Marlo works at a Boutique Bank, one of a group of small Banks with few employees that, in general, do not really do anything. They are usually started by a few "old-timers" with decent connections who want to create an environment that reminds them of the days when they could punch their secretaries in the face and make Analysts work six-hundred-hour shifts in nothing but their boxers with their thighs duct-taped together. While they might succeed in creating this environment, they fail miserably at Banking.

The waitress runs off, still laughing, to charge Marlo's card, and we throw our forks at him in revulsion. When she

returns, Marlo signs the receipt and on the back of the customer copy, we see in her dainty handwriting: *"212-555-6685.
Tell your friend to call me. XX, Heather. P.S. Thanks for the
laugh, WaMu."*

Marlo is now officially known as WaMu.

While Investment Banks have more history to them, the
prestige of PE firms and Hedge Funds depends strictly on
their size. Though their businesses are different, both make
more money with more capital.

Imagine for a second that you decide to start your own
Hedge Fund with the $5,000 that your grandmother willed to
you when she passed away (my condolences). So you, Retard,
LLC, are now a Hedge Fund that is taking various positions
in the market. The thing is (at the writing of this book) you
can only buy around ten shares of Google stock, and then
your funds are exhausted. In this scenario, when a Google
developer figures out time travel in his "Twenty Percent"
spare project time and the stock goes up by 50 percent,
you've still only made $2,500—maybe a big deal to you, but
I left that much in a cab one time.*

---

* Sadly, there are people who work with this scale of capital, but they are
not Bankers, they are called day traders. Day traders sit at home all day
long in sweatpants eating Doritos, watching CNBC, and talking to other
high school dropouts on Internet chat rooms with the goal of getting that
one "hot stock pick" that will finally make them enough money to buy
braces for their hideous thirteen-year-old daughter.

Baller-Ass Funds

I got my acceptance call from the partner at the PE firm I'm moving to while I was on the street walking to a friend's apartment. I answered the unrecognized number with my work tone, and the partner spoke with the confidence of an invincible man. Even over the street noise, it was weird, like hearing my own voice played back to me.

"Welcome to the team," he said. I could distinctly hear the giggle of a girl just old enough to not be his daughter.

I also heard a splash and the bubbles of a Jacuzzi, and I pictured him on the phone on some exotic island, taking a break from getting a hot stone massage to laze by a pool and make a few work calls.

The fund I'm going to be joining manages more than $25 billion. It's in an elite set of funds, most of whom manage over $10 billion, whose moves make the earth shake. These Hedge Funds and PE firms are buying out brands whose jingles are ingrained in everyone's memory and taking positions that could break the economy.

Notable Institutions:

*PE**

—*Blackstone, Kohlberg Kravis Roberts & Co. (KKR), Texas Pacific Group (TPG), Thomas H. Lee, Warburg Pincus, The Carlyle Group*

* Bain Capital has been removed from this group because of its affiliation with Bain Consulting.

Hedge Funds:

—*Citadel, DE Shaw, Qantas, Fortress, AQR, Cerberus, Renaissance Technologies, SAC Capital, Och-Ziff*

Pretty Good Funds

After I hang up with the partner, I'm reminded of a kid, Dave, from my eating club at school. We all thought he was just another normal Princeton guy, not particularly a standout, but someone who had piggybacked his way into the club off a few well-connected kids he had managed to become friends with. Turns out it was all an act. Someone eventually ended up getting close enough to Dave to be invited to his house, and get this: Dave was poor.

When the friend came back to school, word spread like wildfire across campus. At Dave's house, his friend had spotted what became our go-to term for anything shitty, an AGP: aboveground pool. From then on, everything mediocre was an AGP. Tufts? AGP. "Yo, that Toyota your mom drives is sooo AGP," we'd say, even if her car was a Lexus.

Pretty Good Funds, those who generally manage between $500 million and $10 billion or manage more but lack prestige, still count as Hedge Funds or PE firms, technically, but like AGPs, they're not really that fun to be in because they're so small.

Notable Institutions:

PE
—Hellman & Friedman, Clayton Dubilier & Rice (CD&R),
    Providence Equity Partners, Welsh Corson,
Hedge Funds
—Maverick Capital, Millennium Partners, TPG-Axon

Not Funds at All

I try to think of something worse than Dave's AGP, and I can't come up with much. I recall the stories I've heard of underprivileged communities and how they often use fire hydrants or sprinklers as makeshift pools. That seems maybe worse.

There's a great number of Hedge Funds and PE firms under $500 million, and to me, they're all naked little children playing giddily in spurts of water shooting out of a hydrant. These funds may seem happy, but not only are they insignificant, they're depleting otherwise better served resources.

Notable Institutions: None.

In finance, the institutions you work at dictate almost everything about your life. They determine what people think of you and, more important, what you think about yourself. You can either be like WaMu—skipping around in your neighbor's sprinkler, holding up your debit card so the bar code doesn't get wet. Or you can be like me—the ex–Bulge

Bracket, PE guy—hanging out by a grotto in the South of France, getting comped drinks served to you by a pantyless cocktail waitress.

COMMENTS FROM leveragedsellout.com

Wachovia has the best investment bank around—even better than Goldman and Morgan, combined!

Where else can you get a guy who worked his way up from his father's pig farm making a million bucks a minute?

Or a guy who dropped out of high school who worked his way up from teller to repro-room assistant?

I always throw up a W symbol on my chest when meeting my Wachovia peeps. Everyone else is just a poser . . .

WACHOVIA FOR LIFE!!!

POSTED BY ANONYMOUS, MAY 31, 3:21 P.M.

All comments are real and unedited.

CASE STUDY: THE BOUTIQUE

This is the story of Todd, a misguided soul, and Prescott, the guy who set him straight.

The tall, blond, athletic young man presented himself first. "Hi. I'm Prescott Moncrief," he said, extending his hand with a well-practiced smile and MBA eye lock, still debating whether he ought to have included his roman numeral (III) in his introduction.

"'Sup man, I'm Todd," responded the other, grabbing Prescott's formally outstretched hand around the thumb, forcefully wringing it, and releasing it with a loud snap that only he had generated. Todd then used the same hand to clumsily tuck in the loose pieces of his non-slim-fit shirt into his slightly baggy, pleated trousers while attempting to un-successfully balance a dip cup in the other.

"So Todd, what do you do here in the city?" inquired Prescott, regaining comfort but still frazzled by the urban handshake. He couldn't help but feel awkward as he shuffled his feet, trying to dodge the stray dip splitlets that might sully his new driving shoes.

"I work for a boutique investment bank," responded Todd cockily, smirking and now pulling his pants up over his temporarily retreated beer gut, making it clear that this was one of those hardcore New York manorexia and exercise weeks.

He would be spilling out of his pants next week no problem after this weekend's depression gorge.

"Oh, I see," replied Prescott as if the pieces had started to fall together. "I work in finance too. I work at Goldman Sachs," replied Prescott, suppressing the urge to rip Todd's confidence to bits. He had just put together Todd's life story:

> *Todd grew up in a wealthy family in upstate New York or Connecticut, went to a state school (Tufts/Northwestern included) or Second Tier Ivy like Cornell or Penn, where he was a 3.0–3.3 GPA econ major and borderline drug addict. Nearing graduation, he incessantly tried to interview with every bank on The Street, cold-calling the ones that didn't bother responding to his pathetic résumé, and then botched the few interviews he actually managed to get by forgetting the impact of goodwill on net income. Finally, dear daddy, the savior, swooped in and landed Toddkins a position at aforementioned "boutique," where he has since toiled obsequiously under the tutelage of hasbeen "heyday" bankers.*

Todd paused and collected himself. "Yeah, I mean, I just really wanted to be closer to the deals, you know. Get more exposure."

"Yes, of course. Very understandable," replied Prescott, feigning belief and interest. He told himself he was above mocking his feeble conversation partner, but he could not resist.

"So, done any big mergers lately? I hear Joe's Deli bought a liquor store in the Bronx." Prescott snickered.

Todd instantly turned fiery red. The chip on his shoulder was throbbing so hard it was actually beginning to appear as a translucent mass. "F*ck you, man. We just did a huge IPO of this trucking company in Ohio!" retorted Todd angrily, immediately realizing the idiocy of his statement. He muttered something, fumbling to recover, and then finally got out, "Well, I work really closely with our partners who have great connections in the industry!"

Prescott just shook his head in disbelief. "Todd," Prescott said calmly. "I'm going to refrain from further ruining your few hours away from the testosterone-driven madhouse you call work. Actually, I think I hear your out-of-date, boxy BlackBerry going off right now. That's your MD. I think he wants you to bring him another coffee. But keep 'trucking,' they might even promote you to Excel next month!"

Prescott paused, basking in his pedigree.

"And I'm going to do you one more favor," continued Prescott, unable to restrain himself. He reached into his pocket and removed his wallet. He flipped it open and grandiosely pulled out a business card. "Take this. Put it in your pocket, and maybe then you'll get some small sense of what it's like to work at a real bank. And maybe you'll finally be able to pull a half-decent girl instead of that hog over there waiting for you."

Todd could do nothing more than gape into the space Prescott had just occupied. Memories of mediocrity inundated and paralyzed him. Images of report cards with Bs, mid-1300 SATs, cute-face-but-overweight girls, and trophy chests with only JV letters ricocheted off his mind's eye and piled together in one big subpar hunk. Then the logic hit him like a blow to the gut—he was mediocre, and so Boutique Investment Banks must be too. The one thing he had thought separated him from the schmoes actually just illustrated how much of a schmo he really was. He sank to his knees and let his head and prematurely thinning hair fall into his hands. He was a joke.

Case Study Takeaway: Boutiques are cool in SoHo . . . not in Midtown.

PERFORMANCE REVIEW #1

1. In a WWF-style cage match, what would be the order of elimination (first to last) of the following combatants?

    a. Trader

    b. I-Banker

    c. PE Guy

    d. Hedge Funder

The correct answer: c,d,b,a. Explanation: C gets knocked out early on while trying to buy out the WWF. D loses to B only because B is so strung out on Red Bull he bites D's jugular. A of course wins based on experience and innate mastery of the figure-four leg lock.

2. You recently came into a multimillion-dollar inheritance. Who do you *not* trust to manage your money?

    a. A company whose name consists of two or more Jewish surnames.

    b. A firm with a Web site that looks like it was designed by a Down syndrome baby.

    c. Johnnie Chan.

    d. A bank that charges ATM fees.

The correct answer: d.

3. Aboveground Pool : Olympic Size :: $500MM Hedge Fund : _____

    a. Citadel

    b. CD&R

    c. Goldman Sachs

    d. Houlihan Lokey

The correct answer: a.

4. True or false: Underwriters are pimps.

The correct answer: True.

5. Mark the following items of a portfolio as long/short:

    a. Barack Obama

    b. Digital Music

    c. Uggs

    d. Shia LeBeouf

The correct answers:
Barack Obama (short)
Digital Music (long)
Uggs (short)
Shia LeBeouf (long)

6. You come home from work and your two-hundred-pound girlfriend explodes upon you with glee as she tells you she's reduced her weight by one hundred bps. How much does she weigh now?

The correct answer: 198 pounds (short).

People

FACT #5

Georgetown? I wouldn't let my maids' kids go there.

Schools

SCHOOLS AND BANKING follow the same basic patterns as all things in nature. For example, look at the most discrete element of matter: the atom. In basic orbit, the electrons of an atom cannot jump from any given energy level to another; they are restricted to the orbitals in which they belong, their ground state.

Finance operates by these same rules. Kids from middle-tier schools stay at middle-tier Banks and Top-Tier kids stay in the Top Tier. Just like no electron can hop from e1 to e5, there's no Miami of Ohio student who miraculously ends up at a top private equity firm—that shit just doesn't happen. It would be chaos.*

* Of course, electrons do "jump" orbitals, but in finance, this is quite dangerous and actively avoided.

Banker Schools

High School

As far as primary and secondary education are concerned, Bankers now come from various, diverse upper-middle and upper-class schools. Sadly, the days when all Bankers prepped at a proper institution (Exeter, Andover, Hotchkiss, et al.) like I did are over. Some Bankers are still legit, but a large portion went to these places I hear them refer to as "public schools."

College

In the current environment, much more important than prior education is the college or university one attends. Top Banks mainly pull from the highest-ranked institutions, but overall, Banking has a smattering of students from many different schools, as people weasel their way in through family networks and sickening feats of persistence.

Getting an interview at a top Bank can range from being as easy as putting your name down on a list to as difficult as sitting around trying to guess at recruiters' e-mail addresses based on various syntactic schemes (firstname.lastname@ballerbank.com, etc.). Hint: The guy guessing e-mail addresses didn't go to Harvard.

When new Analysts or employees are introduced, their undergraduate institution is without a doubt their main point of distinction. And from this one simple fact, I'm able to deduce a wealth of information about the person in question.

Top Tier

Princeton

School Slogan: "Princeton—We Bringin' Banker Back."

In *This Side of Paradise,* F. Scott Fitzgerald said of my alma mater, "I think of Princeton as being lazy and good-looking and aristocratic." He got two out of three—Princetonians aren't lazy. On the contrary, Tigers work furiously and diligently to ensure their top spots on Wall Street. I imagine F. Scott couldn't make it past first-round Banking interviews and, in his bitterness, made some blanket generalizations.

In my less biased opinion, I think of Princeton as being the consummate Banker school. Elitism, scholarship only for the sake of monetary gain, and a work-hard/ball-hard philosophy are the very bricks that bolster this institution. It brings a tear to my eye just thinking about it.

At the center of the university's social system is a set of upperclassmen eating clubs where students take meals and do beer slides on eighteenth-century mahogany floors. Engineered into this system is an exclusivity that actively prepares students for the careers they are about to embark upon. Hell, the eating clubs are even all neatly lined up in a row on what is known as The Street.

Bicker, which the best eating clubs subscribe to, is Princeton's polished version of fraternity rush. There are also clubs that don't believe in this process and allow potential members to just "sign in." Intuitively, the Bicker clubs are the

Bulge Bracket of The Street and the non-Bicker eating clubs are insignificant. Imagine how effectively a Bank would run if you could just sign your name and become an employee—they'd be as broke as non-Bicker club girls.

But the most compelling part about Princeton is that everyone, regardless of social standing, major, or aspiration, ends up in Banking after graduation, even if it's only for a short spell. Other Ivy League schools go through the motions of offering students postcollegiate opportunities beyond finance, but Princeton appropriately says "fuck that," and rarely lets anyone other than Banks recruit on campus. It's no wonder we've held the number-one spot in *U.S. News & World Report* for the past four years.

At Princeton, there's even a special yearly event known as Reunion. It occurs during graduation, when thousands of alumni come back to campus to party, wear orange, and make sure that if somehow, someone didn't manage to land a job in finance, they can finally get a job in "the family business."

Harvard

School Slogan: "Harvard—With Great Power Comes Great Responsibility."

Meeting someone from Harvard, they will undoubtedly display faux modesty and say something along the lines of, "Oh, I went to school in Boston." I imagine they want me to guess MIT, just so they can say "Harvard" proudly in response, but instead, I say something like, "Hmm. You really look like a Northeastern kind of guy. BU, maybe?" This puts them in their place, and they will scramble away, crying crimson tears all over the floor.

But, to their credit, Harvard's name universally carries the most prestige. That's why people "ooh" and "aah" even when someone's second cousin ends up at Harvard podiatry school, and that's why Banks like having Harvard kids on their desks.

Harvard has its own set of exclusive upperclassmen clubs known as final clubs, but they're much more focused on politics, erudition, and pomp than on facilitating careers as millionaires. In fact, there is a legend about the Porcillian Club, known as one of the most exclusive clubs (along with A.D.), that says, "If members of the Porcillian do not earn their first million before they turn thirty, the club will give it to them." To which I say: "If you haven't made your first million by the time you're thirty, you should fucking *kill yourself*." One can only hope they have begun to account for inflation.

The thing about Harvard is that it's perpetually trying to give students the impression that they're destined for something better, more glamorous, or more creative than finance. One look at *02138* (their zip code, how *90210*), a magazine geared toward Harvard alumni, and it's obvious that the university is trying to sell students on the notion that they could and should be the next Natalie Portman, John Roberts, or a writer for *The Simpsons*.

But in the broader scheme of things, these people are just entertainers and counsel in the grand court of life. Who wants to be a jester when he could be more like another Harvard alumnus, Lloyd Blankfein (CEO of Goldman Sachs), and be The King?

Wharton
School Slogan: "Wharton—University of Pennsylvania"
Based on their curriculum, I originally had Wharton slotted in the Vocational Banker Schools section below, but some stubborn fact-checker at my publisher made a huge fuss and cited various "facts" to prove that Wharton was indeed a Top-Tier Banker school. Not coincidentally, the fact-checker happened to be a Wharton alum. Figures.

I'll concede that a lot of prestigious Bankers do come from Wharton. But the fact that it is attached to the University of Pennsylvania is Wharton's biggest and most tragic downfall. In and of itself, Wharton is a fairly exclusive place, but the nature of its being lumped together with a big, ugly mass of mediocrity creates insecure, overcompensating alumni. As a result, you will *never* hear a Wharton grad admit he went to UPenn. Even if he snuck in through the back door to Wharton after his second year, he will undeniably declare "Wharton" when he meets you, like a leper proudly extending his one good finger to shake. I see the rest of your disfigured hand, buddy, and it's revolting.

Second (Chip on My Shoulder) Tier

Stanford

School Slogan: "Stanford— ~~West~~ Sell Side 4 Life!"

Stanford is a school on the nonBanker side of the States that's full of jocks, hippies, and programmers who fancy themselves "entrepreneurs." Eek. The only reason Stanford appears on this list is because its sheer size ensures that a certain percentage of students end up in finance. For the most part, though, these kids end up in the satellite offices (see "Fact #12—It's all Jersey to me" for additional detail), Boutique Banks by the Bay struggling for business, or interning at floundering VC firms.

Stanford, here's a piece of advice: if you want to increase the prestige of your school, funnel some of the massive funds you spend on athletes to provide scholarships to potential Bankers. Wait . . . actually, no future Banker comes from a family that needs money *that* desperately. Well, at least you've got Michelle Wie.

Yale

School Slogan: "Yale—Overvalued."

Yale is frequently considered among the ranks of Princeton and Harvard but should not be. Yale is indeed an academically pedigreed school with a set of deliciously elite secret societies, but instead of concentrating their efforts on joining the ranks of high finance, something causes Elis to focus on careers in civil service, legislation, and thespianism. It's difficult to imagine what would compel someone thusly—perhaps they yearn to return to the squalor they experienced in New Haven?

Anyway, Yale does produce a few Bankers a year, but the closest it gets to the glamour of Wall Street is via the investments of its large endowment, run by David Swensen, a University of Wisconsin–River Falls graduate (ouch . . . risky!).

Massachusetts Institute of Technology (MIT)
School Slogan: "Small. Yellow. Different."

I don't know much about MIT except that it is the world's foremost nerd kibbutz. Students band together under the premise that looks, fashion, pop-culture knowledge, and hygiene should take a backseat to Integrated Circuits. This lasts for three years, until all the computer science, math, and physics geeks get to senior year and realize they need to figure out how to fund the skyrocketing cost of their World of Warcraft addictions—a lifestyle the salary of a lowly engineer can no longer support.

As such, many MIT students figure they'll apply their in-depth knowledge of signal processing and algebraic topology to go into finance and be quants. Some students are able to get these positions, but many others end up realizing they're not quite as "quant" as they originally thought and end up in generalist positions. They often consider themselves superior to other Bankers because of their loose understanding of neural networks and Fourier space, but their preconceived notions about their intelligence are, appropriately, artificial.

That kind of knowledge actually tends to hinder a true Banker more than help him.

Third (Shit) Tier

Cornell

School Slogan: "Cornell—Mediocrity Delivered."

Most people don't realize that three out of the seven of Cornell's undergraduate schools are *publicly* funded, but most people do realize that all seven are lucky to have been part of whatever blunder placed them in the Ivy League. Cornell produces top "scholars" in two things: agriculture and hoteling; everyone else is stoked on whatever finance job or gorge they're lucky enough to land in.

Dartmouth

School Slogan: "Dartmouth—Keystone Light Meets Finance Light."

I imagine the dumbest, hokeyest, frattiest kids from Princeton hidden away in the mountains of New Hampshire, and I see Dartmouth. They have secret societies, but their names are things like Sphinx and Dragon, which sound more like creatures out of Magic: The Gathering than any social network that's worth being tapped into.

One would think that being so painfully isolated, "dudes" would study hard to try and get jobs in finance so they could move into civilization. But instead, they opt to float down the

Connecticut River on oversized inner tubes (Tubestock—not a lie) and hit on ugly chicks who are way too into ice hockey.

Duke
School Slogan: "Duke—Down Here, Guys!"
Duke is prime evidence to the fact that merely being affluent and white in America can no longer thrust one into the upper echelons of the finance industry. Sadly for the Blue Devils, competition now demands that one also be intelligent.

Just like Duke is *almost* an Ivy League and its students *almost* made the top 5 percent of their class, Duke Bankers can *almost* make it into the most elite PE firms or Hedge Funds, but fail. What a heartbreaking existence of perpetual slightly above-averageness.*

Vocational Banker Schools

In many public high schools, I've heard that there is a group of kids who leave in the middle of the day to go study vocational arts such as plumbing, HVAC, and cosmetology. The kids who go to Vocational Banker Schools also miss real school to learn something you're meant to learn on the job,

* Many people refer to Duke as "The Princeton of the South." This doesn't refer to Princeton University, but to Princeton County Community College (P3C), which opened up its first satellite branch in Durham, NC, and named it after its most notable alumnus—some dude named Duke.

except they pay about $200k because they think it'll help them get into the industry. At least the students who study plumbing learn hard skills and gain connections to a union; all Vocational Banker School graduates have to show for their efforts is a Bachelor of Business Administration (BBA) degree, which no one has heard of or cares about at all.

New York University (Stern School of Business)
School Slogan: "NYU—Bright Lights, No Future."

You'd think that being situated in New York City, the epicenter of finance, NYU would be a great Banker institution. Proximity suggests that countless finance gods would claim NYU as their alma mater and that the school would easily feed its graduates into the top spots on Wall Street. That's just the kind of illogical thinking Stern relies on to stay afloat.

Sadly, the few NYU grads who do make it onto The Street deal with their school like a horrible one-night stand, wiping it from their memories. While recruiting, they will treat Stern candidates like illegitimate offspring, suddenly becoming awkward and saying: "It isn't mine."

University of Michigan (Ross School of Business)
School Slogan: "Ross: Dress for Less."

The Ross School of Business was founded at the University of Michigan (one of "the nation's top state schools," whatever that means) by Stephen Ross, a real-estate developer. I can't help but find this odd—like a nurse opening up a med school. The few UMich kids who do finagle their way onto

The Street demonstrate a similar level of grooming—their brains are overloaded with trivial facts and formulas, but they never quite grasp the overarching concepts that matter.

Carnegie Mellon University (Tepper School of Business)
School Slogan: "CMU—Nerdy, Yet Dumb."
CMU is on this list because not only is its business school in the shadow of Wharton, its engineering school is in the shadow of MIT—a double whammy of rejection that creates a student body with supremely low self-esteem. What ends up happening in this situation is that the engineering nerds take whatever few finance jobs are available at CMU and the Tepper School of Business kids are left with the ever-shameful IT consulting.

Indiana University (Kelley School of Business)
School Slogan: "Indiana—Banker from the Breadbasket."
How the fuck did this get on the list?

Other schools Bankers *might* come from: Vanderbilt, Tufts, UVA, Columbia.

Non-Banker Schools

There are also many categorically non-Banker universities. Like financial aid, I only really know about these schools through hearsay and folklore, so I can't be 100 percent certain they even exist. Let's hope they do not.

Swarthmore / Oberlin / Haverford / Carleton
School Slogan: "<picture of Che Guevara>"

There are many schools across the country that are part of a network known as the "small liberal arts schools." I believe you end up at one of these places when you can't pass Calculus and vaguely understand but are still obsessed with Milan Kundera. Know one thing though—when someone says to you: "I went to a small, liberal arts school," that means "I make $40k a year, gross." Gross.

Brown
School Slogan: "What Can Brown Do for You? Nothing."

At Brown, grades and GPAs are optional. At Banks, Brown graduates are not only "optional" but "highly discouraged." I did meet someone from Brown once, and he told me how their classes were "Satisfactory/No Credit"–based. I thereby assigned him and everyone else from Brown "No Credit" for life.

Business Schools

Harvard Business School
School Slogan: "HBS—Nothing Else Matters."

There is officially only one proper Banker business school: HBS (Harvard Business School). Supposedly, other institutions do hand out MBAs, but they are not even worth being acknowledged.

International Schools

While the rest of the world struggles to keep up with the United States in terms of cultural and political development, their universities lag even farther behind. I attribute this largely to the concept of public higher education systems, which, by giving opportunity to poor people, essentially strips a university of all its Banker potential.

The United Kingdom comes close with Oxford, Cambridge, and the London School of Economics (which sounds elite purely based on the use of the word *Economics*). Canada, as expected, has nothing to offer. The Indian Institute of Technology (IIT) might actually be leading this pack with its notoriously genius graduates who can conjure fire out of thin air and program computers to cure AIDS. We don't really like them in Banking though, as these skills have more utility back in the Third World.

FACT #6

You're just not the right *fit* for us.

Selection

MILLIONS OF PEOPLE try to land jobs in Banking every year, hoping to get their paws on the immeasurable rewards that the business offers. As such, financial institutions must implement extremely rigorous recruitment processes to ensure that the brightest minds are lured in and the garbage is kept out of sniffing distance.

I went back to school for on-campus recruiting this year. It was hard to imagine that I could feel any cooler than when I was a student, but as an alumnus working at a Bulge-Bracket Bank, I did.

I felt a rush as soon as I stepped into our auditorium and saw hundreds of students buzzing around, trying eagerly to grab the attention of anyone in finance. They ran around like chickens with their heads cut off, regurgitating the same slew of questions to anyone who would listen. I took my post behind our table and spoke with an enthusiastic but aloof candor.

"What's the work/life balance like in Banking?" I'd be asked.

Immediately and sternly I would respond: "The consulting firms are in the back."

"How does your Bank compare to the others?"

"We're better. Here, take a water bottle." And, laden with paraphernalia and pamphlets, the young sycophants would either scurry along or loiter by our table hoping we might let some insider information slip.

Girls came by the booth, and they were starry-eyed. I suspect many weren't even interested in finance but just hoping to bathe for a second in our presence. They received both a water bottle and my business card, just in case they "had any questions."

The Lure

I had to be courteous to everyone, regardless of qualifications, but I didn't particularly feel bad about instilling false hopes; that's what we do. We entice students from all backgrounds to apply so we have the lowest acceptance rates, even if that means my spending five minutes humoring some dumb Spanish major who doesn't have a chance in hell.

Someone in East Asian Studies came by the table for information and, unsolicited, started to describe how learning Chinese was extremely "analytical" and applicable to finance. I tried to see the connection for a minute, and then I just started picturing this guy with a half-bald head and ponytail doing a discounted cash flow analysis with a huge paintbrush, ink, and a scroll out of *Crouching Tiger, Hidden Dragon*.

The Hose

Résumés and Cover Letters

After we get everyone on campus to apply, we filter for only the highest-quality candidates. This process consists of reviewing résumés and cover letters and then conducting a set of interviews, which leaves the majority of applicants with nothing but an unrealized dream and a Bank-branded Nalgene—a lifelong reminder of just how great things could have been.

A large part of the résumé and cover letter screening is done by Human Resources, but since I was on campus, I got to see a lot of them. Perhaps I took my Banking intuition for granted, but glancing at the documents we received, I couldn't help but scratch my head and realize that a significant number of people have no idea how to apply for anything. Here were some common faux pas.

COVER LETTERS

❑ Overtemplating: Cover letters are meant to be rigid and structured, but many people get lazy, write one cover letter, and simply do a "find/replace" to change the firm name. This practice is mostly transparent and often another firm's name will not get properly replaced and these artifacts will show up, black-balling an applicant from the entire industry.

❑ Honesty: I've seen cover letters in which otherwise strong candidates will feel this odd desire to be brutally honest, using them as some sort of means for emotional expression. Do you really think I care that "you're not 100 percent sure" but "curious to learn more about finance"? Why are you telling me about your stupid study-abroad trip to Chile? I'm sorry your mother died freshman year and that's why you got a B− in POL 210. I truly am. Ding!

RÉSUMÉS

❑ Typos: How people can submit résumés with typos in them is completely beyond me. You think a Bank would hire someone who doesn't know *it's* from *its*,

INSTAOFFER

IDEAL COVER LETTER

Dear Sir/Madam,

I am applying for the Analyst position with Lehman Brothers' Investment Banking division. I am steadfast in my dedication to a career in finance and am certain I would be a tremendous asset to Lehman Brothers.

I have read *The Wall Street Journal* cover-to-cover every day since I was seven and am able to recite most articles from memory. I know I have the eye for perfection and artistic vision to create truly immaculate pitch books. I am Microsoft-Certified in Excel, and I know all the shortcut keys (alt-i then r, to insert a new row) by heart. Furthermore, I consider myself a whiz with numbers and have no doubt that I would be able to build robust models and complete precise calculations for Lehman Brothers.

Most important, however, I want to stress how willing I am to do "anything for the team." I realize the possibility of long hours exists in such a position, and I am ready to work as hard as necessary. I have been practicing staring at a computer monitor for extended hours, I can currently sit motionless in front of a screen for twenty-eight hours, and I am improving daily.

I appreciate your taking the time to review my application and hope you indeed "go to bat" for me. Please contact me with any further questions you may have at timsmith@ameritrade.com.

Sincerely,
Tim Smith

DAMN, IT FEELS GOOD TO BE A BANKER

forgets periods, and misuses the first-person reflex-
ive? No. But as you might say: keep that "between you
and I."

❑ Passive Voice: Bankers *do* shit. We *make* shit happen.
Things do not happen *to* us. It was not raining the
other day. We *made* it rain, bitch.

❑ Overzealous Hobby Listing: It is sometimes nice to
know that a candidate plays tennis, is a decorated
triathlete, and enjoys reading *The Economist*—these
things add color. That said, no one cares that you
are internationally ranked in badminton, volunteer
at your local soup kitchen, and play Everquest—
these things are disgusting.

❑ "Forgetting" SAT scores/GPA: A very common practice by people who know that their stats are unimpressive. Heads up: we realize it too, and you're
getting hosed!

Interviews

A close friend of mine had a younger brother on campus
who was applying for finance jobs, so I agreed to impart
some advice about interviews.

He was nervous, but I sat him down and explained, "Interviews, like life, are based on two things: looks and attitude."

We went through his wardrobe and picked out a decent
suit and tie and paired them with an impressive leather portfolio to sheath fifteen copies of his résumé. And then we

fell over laughing as we saw his roommate leave in khakis, a button-down, and a five-inch-wide tie for his Amnesty International interview. I could already envision the poor, starving people of Myanmar turning away aid because that dude's outfit was more painful than any of the parasites they were infested with.

I stood the young Banker-to-be in front of the mirror and instructed him to *visualize* himself on Wall Street. He made a few pathetic attempts at an "M&A snarl" and eventually got something close. I let him hold my BlackBerry for a moment so he could feel the surge of pulling it out of his pocket and shooting it at the mirror. A quick "pew pew," and he was enamored; I had to wring it from his hands.

We went over the interview vocabulary. He loved every Bank's "culture" and was fascinated by their "mission," "vision," and "corporate philosophy." He lived for "projects," and any structured problem-solving. Despite the fact that he worked on every problem set alone, he could not stand environments that were not "team-oriented."

He asked about the difference between "fit" and "technical" interviews, which I told him was irrelevant. A well-delivered response that utilizes the interview vocabulary is appropriate for any question.

Example:
Question: "Why might a company choose to issue debt vs. equity?"

*Answer: "Oh, I just love working on projects! Everything
I do, I break down into discrete, actionable tasks with
timelines and goals. I'm tremendously diligent and won't
stop until I've seen a project to completion."*

Capital structure doesn't mean shit if you're convincing.

I even took a moment to prep him on Trading interviews.
I snuck up behind him and screamed, "What's 14 times 59?!"
And by the fifth time, he was able to immediately and accurately reply "826, asshole," and huff excitedly like a Trader. I
also gave him a large, manly phone, and he slammed it down
hard, proving he could handle himself in any situation on
The Floor if necessary.

He had even prepared a joke, just in case:

*"What was the best part of Playboy Enterprises (PLA)'s
IPO?"*
"The pitch book."

Not bad.

During an interview, it is undoubtedly asked: "Do you
have any questions?" I heard of a kid who once responded
"No" in this situation, and he was instantaneously black-
balled from every Bank on The Street. He could have made
up *anything,* and it wouldn't have mattered, but he didn't.
His little sister tried to get a job in financial services consulting three years later, but the myth was still alive and she, too,
got hosed from everywhere.

We reviewed the only other three relevant questions. "What is the effect of goodwill on net income?" "What is the correlation between bond prices and inflation?" and "If you had to use one word to describe you, what would it be?" To which he was to respond: "None," "Inverse," and *"Driven,"* respectively.

The Close

My protégé ended up making it through several Super Saturdays—the special days where a Bank conducts three hundred interviews in eight hours—and received a handful of offers.

He was no longer the orphan looking for a family; the Banks were competing for *him.* He received personal calls from MDs, and was getting hourly e-mails from Jen Yang, an alumna working at a Boutique Bank, who was asking him out for coffee in case he "had any questions." That must be everyone's code word, because on the coffee date, he discovered that her Boutique was coercing Jen to sleep with guys to get them to accept their offers. I instructed him to partake, but, of course, not to go work at her Bank.

With fairly equivalent salaries and notions of culture,

mission, and philosophy now out the window, he did what any Banker does; he went with the most prestigious one.

Post-Undergrad Recruiting

While on campus, I had a second to reflect on the differences between undergraduate and later-stage recruiting. From friends already in MBA programs, I knew the process was similar but that MBAs are much better trained, professional ass-kissers who elbow and box out competitors if given any opportunity to network.

From my experience applying for PE jobs, I took a moment to curse headhunters. "Search consultants," as they euphemize themselves, make money by brokering deals between Banks and recruits; and like arms dealers, their tactics are morally abject but can lead to a fairly sizable income.

I heard a very telling story from a Prop Trader about headhunters. One day, he picked up his phone and gave his usual warm greeting: "Trading. What?" The person on the other line claimed to be a FedEx delivery man who just needed the name and number of someone on the desk to sign for a package. The Trader gave a colleague's contact info and fifteen minutes later his friend received a series of calls from a headhunter with various "opportunities." Not only did they find the headhunter, tie him to the Wall Street bull, and hurl rocks at him, they also beat the shit out of the next three FedEx delivery guys, just to be safe.

$$$

When my work was completed, I left on-campus recruiting knowing I was able to help Banking harvest the nation's top talent. I had done a noble service.

Additionally, two beautiful undergraduate girls did *me* a noble service after they recognized me out partying, still in my suit and my Bank's nametag. Turns out, they "had some questions" after all.

CASE STUDY: FITZWATER

This is the story of what to say to people who fall short of their dreams.

Recruiting for Banking reminded me a lot of Bicker, the rush process for Princeton's exclusive coed eating clubs. Just like a Bank on Wall Street, which eating club you belonged to at Princeton defined your entire social experience and self-worth. "What club were you in?" is without fail the first question asked when random Princeton alumni meet, and just as "Piper Jaffray" isn't a great answer in Banking, neither is "Cloister," one of Princeton's crappier eating clubs.

Bicker is more formal than most fraternity rushes, and as in finance recruiting, people interview you and then discuss and ridicule every minute detail of your life behind closed doors. Bicker is held during the spring semester, in the middle of sophomore year, which gives students enough time to find the club of their dreams and induces freshman girls to sleep with as many upperclassman club members as possible. It's pretty genius.

But there's a weird kink in the Bicker system: You're technically allowed to bicker multiple times. The next year, in the fall, juniors can bicker again and try to gain acceptance. You can even try a third time the following spring. It makes no sense at all to allow these rejects to get up to bat a second time, and very few succeed. Those who do—mostly girls who've started dating guys in the club—are treated like second-class citizens for their tenure as club members and the rest of their lives.

At Ivy, my eating club, there was this kid, Ryan Fitzwater, who bickered for the first time in the spring, along with a few hundred other sophomores. He was a disaster. Ivy is a selective place, but it's not impossible to get in. Have a father who's a famous U.S. politician? Mother get quoted regularly in the *Wall Street Journal*? Last name written on our library? This was all it really required. Beyond these simple qualities, not too much mattered, except that you weren't a raging douchebag.

Fitzwater, however, *was* a raging douchebag and pissed off all ten of his interviewers. A short, fat little guy from North Carolina, he was overt about his connections and mentioned repeatedly how his father had donated several million dollars to Princeton. You aren't supposed to *say* that kind of shit, Fitzwater, we just *know* it. Naturally, he got hosed.

Fitzwater then gave bickering Ivy a second attempt in the fall of his junior year, only to get hosed yet again.

At that point, we all thought it was over with him—that he might have gotten the message.

But then, around December, Fitzwater actually came back to the club for a party. Gutsy. Like a little kid who just won't realize no one wants to play with him, he kept trying to schmooze and brownnose with everyone. "I'm really excited about bickering again this spring," he'd say. "Was just having an off couple days the past two times around."

Right, Fitzwater. Sure.

That night, Fitzwater got absolutely smashed. He was playing Robopound, the intelligent man's version of quarters we employ at Princeton, and losing severely; he couldn't bounce a quarter to save his life. After twelve or so losses, he started stumbling around like a drunk idiot, screaming obscenities and throwing things—acceptable behavior for an Ivy member, but not Fitzwater.

To top it off, he began groping girls on the dance floor. It wasn't solicited, so it came off creepy as opposed to appropriate. The bouncers ended up forcefully removing Fitzwater from the club and physically throwing him out the back door. On his knees in the grass, he lingered for a moment, grasping longingly in the direction of our mansion. A bunch of us were on the balcony, sipping drinks and enjoying a brisk but relatively warm winter night. The mild weather was a blessing, because we got to watch this pathetic display.

Finally, Fitzwater got up and started to stumble toward the gate, his sobs audible but gradually getting quieter as he got farther away. Our house manager, Ethan, a large, athletic guy, got up off a lounge chair and leaned over the balcony. Plastic cup in hand, he bellowed at the staggering reject: "GOOD LUCK IN THE SPRING, FITZWATER!"

I nearly keeled over from laughter. From then on, that phrase became our go-to whenever anyone was failing at anything in life, even if there was no hope at a second chance. See a guy wearing Old Navy? GOOD LUCK IN THE

SPRING, FITZWATER! Meet someone without a trust fund? GOOD LUCK IN THE SPRING, FITZWATER! The object of derision doesn't even have to be animate; I say it to the Bank of America building every time I pass it.

Most important to the idiom, however, is the delivery. It has to be spoken exactly the way that Ethan said it that night—belted from the gut, as if introducing the starting lineup of a basketball team or announcing a goal during a soccer game on Telemundo. Also in this spirit, the "r" in "spring" is trilled and often drawn out for added effect.

This story yields an important lesson about recruiting in Banking—do not be a raging douchebag, at least not at first. These kinds of people need to be punished. So when a similarly annoying kid gave me his résumé at a career fair, I turned it over and in big, block letters, I wrote: "GOOD LUCK IN THE SPRING, FITZWATER."

He figured out what that meant pretty quickly.

FACT #7

Mergers are a
girl's best friend.

Girls

AS MUCH AS we would like the only girls we interact with to be nineteen, tipsy, and still dressed from their last photo shoot, even Bankers have to mingle with nonmodels. This happens primarily with colleagues, but also when a Banker hits that critical age (forty-five to fifty) when he's done sowing his royal oats. At this point, we need to settle down and find a quality wife with whom we can create and train future financiers.

Banker Chicks

At my apartment, we have a drawer where we keep all the random crap that girls leave behind after we hook up with them. This appears to be a well-known relationship device among women, who frequently call the next day, try to come by, pick up their item, and finagle a date; depending on the weekend, the drawer might either be nearly empty or require an entire extra cabinet.

It's a shrine to New York City's finest women, having been filled with necklaces, earrings, and other personal items. These things often "get left" on bedside tables or "fall out" of purses. Once, a $2,000 handbag itself was "forgotten" and had to be stuffed inside. But over the past two years, three things have remained in that drawer from the first week we moved in. My two roommates and I were all in various training programs, and we each ended up hooking up with a Banker Girl who left something behind.

The three things were: a pencil case, a half-eaten cheeseburger, and a Chanel bracelet.

The Joy Luck Investment Club

The pencil case was left behind by an Asian girl who worked in Fixed Income at UBS; my roommate Gopal hooked up with her. We don't know her name or whether she was Indian or East Asian, but we do know that they bonded over some second-generation plight nonsense. In her stickered-up pencil case was a "Math Counts" pen, a Westinghouse/Intel International Science Fair pin, and a Japanese retractable eraser.

As we became more familiar with finance, we found that this pencil-case girl was part of a clan we named the Joy Luck Investment Club. These are primarily Asian girls who majored in electrical engineering, molecular biology, or some other hard science that leveraged her innate diligence. In engineering, they got out-shined by other, more Asian, Asian girls and ended up seeing if they could regain their dominance in Banking. They can't, and over time, their core personalities erode. Now they can no longer even integrate x^2, and all of their brain power has been allocated to memorizing and being able to recite, verbatim, the entirety of *The Journal.* The economics and repercussions of what they can mindlessly spit out, however, are of absolutely no importance to them. (Side note: $\frac{x^3}{3}$. Still got it!)

The Big Uglies

My Trader roommate, Jon, has virtually non-existent standards. After a day of being on the Trading floor, I don't even think he can see straight when he goes out at night; at least that's the only explanation I can come up with for the monsters he brings home.

The half-eaten cheeseburger was from Kate, a girl in Equities whom Jon met at a sports bar drinking pitchers of Bud Heavy. We slotted her in the group of Banker Girls called Big Uglies, which refers to large, bloated industrial stocks (steel, oil, etc.). Big Uglies played lacrosse, softball, basketball, and rugby in college and got into finance through sports connections and the claim that as a result of their experience in athletics, they'd be great "team players." As investments, Big Uglies aren't "sexy," and neither was Kate.

Urban Legends

The Chanel bracelet belongs to the Banker Girl I brought home, Allison. She is to this day the only attractive Banker Girl I have ever seen and the only one I've ever allowed to hook up with me. In training, she was a captivating, seemingly mythical creature—a Wall Street siren, of sorts. She had "Kappa Alpha THETA!" qualities—sexy but still so pure that every guy felt the need to stop cursing around her. Eyes popped out of heads when Allison made an interest rate joke during a break, and guys nearly fainted when the word *synergy* fell seductively off her lips. Everyone begged to have that girl on his desk. It wouldn't even matter if she was intelligent; anyone would have promptly done her work for her.

Allison came back to the apartment with me after our last training event. She wasn't a particularly challenging conquest, and it was a decent experience by any standards. She maintained a certain aloofness about her in the morning, which I appreciated. I didn't see her again, but my roommates caught a glimpse of her prancing out of the apartment and have since been trying to locate other girls like her on Wall Street. We think there might be a few in Sales, but it's hotly debated whether that actually counts (HR doesn't).

$$$

Of the three* finance girls we hooked up with back then, none came back immediately for her stuff. Allison called, but I didn't pick up, and after ringing through to voice mail, she knowingly didn't leave a message. We think the Joy Luck Investment Club girl was happy to shed a relic of her nerdy, pre-Banker life. And since we figured the Big Ugly would definitely call up at some point demanding the rest of her cheeseburger, we just put it in a Ziploc bag and stuffed all three of their things away in a drawer, the function of which later became more defined; it was an appropriate christening.

As we've spent more time in Banking, we've realized that all girls on Wall Street, regardless of type, have certain things in common. For example:

1. They are all at various stages of the pear—skinny top and bulbous bottom. Thankfully, we had caught the girls at the very beginning of the ballooning. The pear is similar to the Freshman Fifteen—the weight girls gain when they go to college—except it's more like the Banker Thirty, and it all aggressively goes to the ass. All Banker Girls fight ferociously in their few gym hours to combat the pear, but it is futile—remaining seated five sixths of the day could flatten J.Lo's booty into a mushy blob.

* These three groups are indeed distinct, as it's impossible for an Asian girl to be either fat or in Theta.

INSIDER INFO WITH BANKERGRRRRL

Finance? Yeah, I mean it's whatever. I like it. I'm good at math, and I'm learning a lot of great business stuff I'll be able to use in the rest of my life. And I figure, how else would I get to go out and have $500 dinners with my friends and buy $3,000 shoes (and tip my shoe repair guy as well as I do)? There are boys, of course. I was dating this guy Excel, but we're on a break. I'm with PowerPoint now.

Wait. Is it Wednesday? My *Us Weekly* comes on Wednesday!! I haven't eaten in days, and I *can't wait* to hit Equinox with it! Grr ... I really hope that fat bitch doesn't take my favorite elliptical again.

Psst. Wanna know a secret? There're a lot of spikes and lulls with the way the deals work on my desk, so when I'm not busy during the day, I sneak out and go shopping.☺ Just gotta leave your bags with the doorman and get 'em on your way out, girl!!

2. All the emotion, clinginess, and drama that make most females so tremendously inefficient to live with become completely expunged from Banker Girls. What remains feels more like the shell of a girl rather than a girl itself—perhaps a worthwhile friend.

3. The female obsession with fashion is exponentially augmented. Every Banker Chick I've ever met fills any lull in conversation with a discussion of how she is just working in finance as a stepping stone to a job in couture. Some are even on the "business side" of a puny little jewelry company they had started with an equally unartistic friend.*

To their credit, however, if a group of Banker Chicks were to go head-to-head with the editors of *Glamour* in some sort of fashion knowledge contest, I'm certain the Banker ladies would win hands-down. Why? Because no one (*no one*) does due diligence like Bankers, even if it's on ballerina flats and Gucci clutches.

Also, Bankers don't really lose at anything, especially not to some wannabe *Vogue* bitches.

$$\$ \$ \$$$

As it turns out, Kate, the Big Ugly, did eventually come back, just last week. As we predicted, she hadn't forgotten about that cheeseburger and was just busy adjusting to life in The City. She came over one night after work, and, surprisingly, I noticed that she had managed to remain at the same level of thickness. Big Ugly stocks do indeed have relatively slow

* Number of times working in finance has led to a career at Louis Vuitton: 0 (but don't tell them that).

growth. Upon seeing her food, she reacted as one does after finding a lost family heirloom. Impassioned, she fell upon the cheeseburger, and, like a savage, she ate the shit out of that two-year-old gnarliness.

Chicks of Bankers

Banker Chicks are a tragic breed, but the girls that Bankers eventually end up with are a stark contrast. They're beautiful, sophisticated women—ones Banker Chicks futilely ape. Through various dinners, work events, and older friends, I've met several women married to older Bankers. They all seem to share the need for a strong, attractive man who can indulge their every material caprice. Granted, this might be all women, but at least the ones who end up with Bankers succeed in achieving their goal.

These women are selected because their beauty is paired with good stock—ensuring proper lineage is a high priority for Bankers. I mean, how would it look if a guy from Blackstone married a waitress? And just imagine how confused their poor children would be. The little rugrats might even feel empathy for the servers at the country club, and the entire system would deteriorate.

Sitting at a restaurant with a group of MDs or PMs at a Hedge Fund and their wives, I can imagine the women as little girls, opening their soda cans methodically, counting the turns as letters, and aggressively ripping off the tabs when they reached *B*. I bet they hoarded those tabs and put them on a string. "This is my 'I'm gonna marry a Banker' necklace!" they must have said giddily when showing their craft to their mothers.

Chicks of Bankers don't really get assessed based on their employment, but they do tend to group together based on their "passions."

Hot-for-Profit

The Hot-for-Profit girl has a passion for "change." In an existence dedicated to negative net income, she has done one profitable thing in her life: getting herself a Banker man. This girl generally focuses her energy on some negligible NGO, either recycling the old Dolce & Gabbana dresses of Connecticut women or helping provide support to thousands of hurricane victims. The only reason this organization is still afloat, however, is because her husband and often his Bank use it as a tax write-off. Her hobby is cute and endearing in its ineffectiveness, and it's fun to humor, as a novelty.

The Takeover Artist

The Takeover Artist is passionate about her "art." She photographs or paints or sculpts "modern," vomit-inducing oddities; she may even fancy herself and her little roman à clef to be literary. But at some point, this girl realizes that she needs someone besides her daddy to keep her from starving, and she turns to a Banker for art supplies.

When I meet a Takeover Artist, I can't help but respect her hypocrisy: she will never sell out her art to be more mainstream; rather, she sells out her tits and ass to get a $15,000 SLR camera with a duffel bag full of lenses she will never figure out how to use.

The CDO (Chief Domesticated Officer)

Some Bankers do end up with women in the corporate world. These women can range from Human Resources or PR girls to middle managers or older female Bankers themselves. This woman's passion was her career; she even chopped her hair at age thirty to look more commanding. She tried to piggyback her way to the top by marrying a more successful man but just got overshadowed. The only bright part of her life now is the two-carat rock on her finger she either proudly displays or hides, depending on her work environment.

The Deal Trophy

My MD is married to a Deal Trophy. Like a Lucite deal toy made of acrylic glass that sits on his desk to commemorate

the completion of a deal, she sits in his house
or stands on his arm and looks pretty.

When I end up around my MD's wife, I
find it impossible not to flirt with her. It's
dangerous, but she's beautiful and
charming in a confident, older woman
way. This appeal is not only what allowed her to snag a Banker but
what makes her perfect to use
when schmoozing with clients.

Talking to her, I find that
her life is complete and ideal.
She is content and has realized all her true passions:
staying at home, doing yogalates, bossing around the maid,
and figuring out innovative methods to blow her Banker
hubby's money on shoes, clothes, and antique accent tables.

Banker Chicks and Chicks of Bankers might not be at the
same level of attractiveness, talk, or dress, but they do share
one thing: a bond forged by their relationships with Banker
men. They're united by an undeniable, mutual truth: their
lives revolve around us.

COMMENTS FROM leveragedsellout.com

As part of that rare subset of "Private Equity" chicks—I can say all of the above applies, especially the struggle between dieting and the really expensive dinners.

And another tip, if you're trying to get your game on, always guess above where you think she actually works . . . if you think she's a Second-Tier Banker Chick, ask her if she works at a Bulge Bracket . . . if you think she's a First-Tier Banker Chick, ask her if she works in private equity . . . hey, we've got to get our kicks from somewhere.

POSTED BY ANONYMOUS, MAY 10, 11:30 A.M.

All comments are real and unedited.

FACT #8

Diversity is one
of our core values.
Race

WALL STREET IS extremely diverse. In other industries, individuals are still slotted into categories based on their race, and they are granted or denied employment opportunities based on the color of their skin. This does not occur in finance. No—we take no part in that kind of backwardness. You see, in Banking, you are judged on important things: what school you went to, how much money you bring into the firm, and what brand your tie is. But once you've passed these tests, you become part of the more important super-race of Bankers—a group no one can be prejudiced against.

Yes, there are a few people who still dream of the days of yore, when all Bankers were blue-blooded and the closest any foreigner got to Wall Street before being hit in the face with a rock was the Statue of Liberty. I imagine that I might have been a bit more "comfortable" in that dynamic, not having to open my mind to understand and accept the heritages of my various colorful colleagues. But, like any good Banker, I prefer a challenge and appreciate the wealth of insight and diverse experiences and culture that all the upper-class American-born minorities bring to our little world.

During my finance tenure, I've worked side by side with Bankers of all cultures. We went through training together, collectively pulled all-nighters, and partied (occasionally) as a single unit. There were, of course, numerous ethnic minorities at my prep school and at Princeton (twelve in total, to be exact), but Banking was the first time the walls were broken down, and I was able to really *get to know* these guys.

My experiences with nonwhite Bankers are numerous, but a few in particular stand out in my mind. These interactions have helped shape my outlook and life and, ultimately, have contributed to my personal growth and overall awareness.

Name:	**Sameer**
Career Goal:	MD
Ethnic Role Models:	Lakshmi Mittal, Kal Penn, Gandhi
Greatest Fear:	Having to eat meat at a work event.
Pet Peeves:	Coming into the office on Saturday, unlevering betas, being called "Bangalore"

My Favorite Memory

Sameer sat next to me, so we became quite close. He was a bright, hardworking guy from Pittsburgh, one of a crew of Indian trailblazers who decided to enter the financial industry instead of medicine.

One thing I noticed early on was that he was always receiving a great deal of pressure from his parents, not only to succeed, but also to "find a good, Indian girl" and "get married." It really seemed to stress him out, almost to the point that he couldn't concentrate on work. To offer some balance, I decided that I would help Sameer "find a hot, white girl" and "get laid." Sameer had just introduced me to the wonders of saag paneer, and, frankly, I felt I owed it to him. I made a few calls and let a couple girls know that I had a dapper Banker friend named "Sam" who was on the market, and the deal sealed faster than a tech IPO in 1998. I've recently moved on to chicken tikka masala, but Sam is still with the same girl I introduced him to way back when. He's not too stressed out, and from what I hear, his parents have stopped pestering him altogether.

Name:	**Michael**
Career Goal:	**Partner at Private Equity Firm**
Ethnic Role Models:	**TBD**
Greatest Fear:	**Asian glowing at a work event**
Pet Peeves:	**Never being able to find an off-the-rack shirt that fits, being called "Chang"**

My Favorite Memory

Chang was as diligent as a barefooted rickshaw driver on a hot summer's day; he could always be counted on. This dependability quickly became apparent, and others took advantage of him, leaving him with much more work than the rest of us. But he never once complained. Chang was quiet and reserved—meditative, even. But he always had this kind of subtle underlying playfulness to him. If he was knee-deep in some analysis, for example, and the staffing manager assigned him something else, he would look over at me. I would have my shoes off and my feet kicked up, and he would snarl, doing this dead-on impersonation of someone really pissed off. Priceless.

One time, I was in the Hamptons, and I got a call from our MD asking me to finish up a few things. I just hate getting sand in my laptop, so I called up the ol' Changster and asked him if he wouldn't mind helping me out quickly. "You're a machine, man! Shouldn't take more than a couple, ten hours," I encouraged him.

I could hear him getting into the huffing part of his impersonation over the phone, and I was curious how that lighthearted snarl might convey itself cellularly. But then he added a new element to his routine, screaming, "FINE. JUST FUCKING STOP CALLING ME CHANG! I'M KOREAN. MY LAST NAME IS LEE," and slamming down the phone.

What a joker! Love that guy.

Name:	**Ari**
Career Goal:	Hedge Fund Manager
Ethnic Role Models:	Stephen Schwarzman, Saul Steinberg, Leon Levy
Greatest Fear:	Falling for a shiksa secretary
Pet Peeves:	Numerous

My Favorite Memory

Apart from me, Ari was the most naturally skilled Banker on our desk. He was smart, with a seemingly unquenchable thirst for business information and married this tenacity with an almost palpable level of greed. It soaked his shirt like his back sweat and was just as noticeable. Awesome. My lust runs deeper for prestige than money, so I didn't entirely grasp Ari's hunger for cash, but I imagined it was the kind that comes about from growing up without boatloads of it. This seemed to correlate well with "Brooklyn"—the town where he was from.

Ari also has very defined goals. From the moment we began working together, he incessantly talked about his dream of running a Hedge Fund. On the way to grabbing lunch, he would relate, at length, how he would one day buy Daniel Loeb's (Third Point LLC) house, torch it, and use it to firebomb Steven A. Cohen's (SAC Capital) residence, leaving him alone as the most badass Jewish Hedge Fund Manager out there. He delivered these statements not as hyperbole, but as inevitabilities he was giving me a preview of.

I respected these musings and realized there could be a mutually beneficial relationship between us. So I sat Ari down one day and told him that in the interim until he became a Hedge Fund Manager, I wanted him to be my personal Trust Fund Manager. He beamed like a son who's just been brought into his father's diamond business. I let him invest only what was in my checking account, but we still had a special moment, and he made me a cool $500k.

Name:	**Natalie**
Career Goal:	Secretary of State
Ethnic Role Models:	Colin Powell, Stan O'Neal, Condoleezza Rice
Greatest Fear:	Having to watch coworkers dance
Pet Peeves:	Being asked, "So, what *is* it like as a minority woman in finance?"

My Favorite Memory

Natalie is the only Banker Chick I can stand being around on a regular basis. She possesses two traits I've never witnessed together in another female Banker: she does good work and she is gorgeous. Through her unique combination of these qualities, she has always managed to get rewarded with compliments and high-profile projects. I back that.

But on one occasion, I heard some other Bankers whispering about how she was a "token" and only got hired because of "affirmative action." I knew that this was not true, and it infuriated me. Natalie was just like a handful of other people who had insta-ins to the firm—her dad was connected. So one day, in a voice loud enough that everyone including Natalie could hear, I stood up at my desk and announced: "Guys. Natalie isn't here because of affirmative action. She is here because her dad is an MD in the Chicago office."

She never thanked me for clearing that up, but I'm sure she was grateful.

$$\$ \$ \$$$

The mathematician Nassim Nicholas Taleb recently wrote a book on what he calls the "black swan theory." There used to be a common conception that all swans were white, and people used the phrase "black swan" for something that could not exist. In the seventeenth century, however, a black swan was discovered in Australia, and as such, Taleb uses the black swan to describe a "large-impact, hard-to-predict, and rare event beyond the realm of normal expectations."

Like the swans we are, there was once a common conception that all Bankers were white. People used the phrase *black Banker* to describe something that could not exist. No one had even imagined a "yellow Banker" or a "brown Banker." Turns out we are even more diverse than swans, and far more striking.

For those unconvinced, just open up any Bank or financial institution's Web site, and you will see numerous pages dedicated to this very subject. And not only is diversity one of our core values—we have the pamphlets to prove it.

Unrelated topic: Chang—if you're reading, we're valuing a couple doctor's-mask companies and could really use your personal expertise to help us decide if this is a market we should jump into. So yeah, any qualitative info beyond the financials would be great.

INSIDER INFO WITH NAIM

Dear Mom / Dad,

Sorry I couldn't make it home this weekend, I got pulled in at the last minute to go speak with a potential client. We might be doing a deal with some record label, "Def Jam," and another MD decided at the last second it was imperative that I attend. Turns out they focus a lot on hip-hop (which you know I hate) so I wasn't too familiar with the company and had to get up to speed really quickly. I'm still in the Healthcare group, but I got to do almost all of the presenting, which is great experience.

Otherwise, things are going well. Everyone is really nice, and I'm learning a lot. There are a few other Harvard guys here, so we're up to all our old antics on the weekends.

I'll try to make it home next weekend, but I also just got pulled in to work on another pitch. "FUBU," I think the company's name is? Anyway, I hope they do medical devices—that's what I've been eager to learn more about.

Talk to you soon,
Naim

COMMENTS FROM leveragedsellout.com

This seems like a good place to post about a personal pet peeve from my own life.

Here's a little bit about my background: went to an Ivy League school, Bulge-Bracket Bank, then a buyout fund where I was promoted to a partner-track position. Oh yeah, I'm also an Asian American who likes to go pick up dinner in order to get some fresh air.

STOP CONFUSING ME WITH THE CHINESE DELIVERY GUY!!!!

I can't begin to tell you how many times this has happened in my career. Just because I'm Asian and I'm carrying a plastic grocery bag through the lobby doesn't mean I'm your fucking delivery guy.

One evening, I was stopped THREE fucking times within a span of twenty-five feet—(1) outside the revolving door, (2) in front of the security desk, (3) in the elevator bank—and asked (1) "Excuse me, are you from . . ." (2) "Wait, where are you going? I ordered sushi." (3) "Hi, my name is . . ."

So if you see an Asian guy with a plastic grocery bag walking through the lobby but dressed in business casual with a BlackBerry clipped to his belt, use some common sense. The Chinese delivery place around the corner didn't start issuing BlackBerries to their delivery people and aren't requiring them to dress business casual so that they can "fit in better."

POSTED BY ANONYMOUS, MARCH 10, 5:10 P.M.

All comments are real and unedited.

FACT #9

Holla back, office!
Support Staff

THERE'S NOTHING QUITE like meeting a random, fellow Banker in a social setting. An instant sense of camaraderie takes over, and the conversation quickly turns to familiar jokes, playful elitism, and a thinly veiled discussion of recent deals. It's like meeting an American in a foreign country and being able to freely bitch about how stupid and backward all the natives are, only you get to do it from the comfort of your homeland, and the "natives" are people who don't work in finance.

Sometimes, however, this feeling will be misplaced. I once met a guy who said he "worked at JPMorgan." *Okay, kinda sweet,* I thought. *I've heard of that.* We chatted in loose terms about the industry and discussed a few trends. But when we got into specifics, his knowledge markedly plateaued.

It was weird. Inspecting him a bit closer, I noticed he had gotten really nervous. His Amstel Light trembled ever so slightly in his hand, sweat beaded up around his temples, and he was treating girls with a strange level of respect, bordering on gratitude. Something was *off.*

Holla back, office!

As I examined him further, a creeping, rhythmic voice got steadily louder in the back of my mind. We played the name game to see if we knew any of the same people—we didn't. As my suspicion heightened, he let a comment slip about getting off work "late" that night, at 7:30 p.m. The voice in my mind instantaneously went from inaudible to nearly bursting my eardrums. "Going going, back back, office office," Tupac boomed, and it all made sense.

I would have spotted it sooner, but he was particularly gifted in his posing. Once it clicked, though, I realized that the dude had "Back Office" written all over him.

In business, the Back Office is any group that isn't actively contributing to the core business of the firm. The Back Office is the support staff—the fluffers whose only purpose is to prepare and assist the real Bankers in the spotlight.

While it varies based on the company, the Back Office generally constitutes departments like Information Technology (IT), Accounting, and Human Resources. They take care of the tasks no one thinks about, and their employees are forgotten and neglected. Every group of friends has a Back Office guy—he's the one who calls and sets up the party but never gets any girls.

Art School (Word Processing/Production)

Word Processing and Production are the parts of the Back Office that Investment Bankers have to interact with the most (Traders and others, not really), as aesthetics are a vital part of any deal. Pitch books, presentations, and other work products must be both accurate and meet the Bank's strict style guidelines because the people who read them, like illiterate four-year-olds, tend to respond to things that are "pretty."

I've become quite friendly with a couple people in WP and Graphics. They're a total departure from the kinds of people I usually deal with, but someone is there, on call, 24/7, and we end up interacting a lot. Once given a task, they'll burrow away somewhere and complete it in perfect solitude. Tania, my WP girl from Queens, can take any Excel chart, sketch, or scribble on the inside of a match book and make it presentable. We might have to iterate on it a few hundred times, but we've got a comfortable level of "don't flip out on me, and I won't flip out on you"–ness going on.

Production (Graphics) then prints, binds, and sends out the documents. Special paper, spiral/comb binding—they make the book reports every child dreams of being able to create. Production at Bulge-Bracket Banks makes Apple's packaging look like one of the brown bags that the Back Office folks bring their lunch to work in.

The guys in WP and Graphics aren't the type to pose as Bankers; they're aloof and too cool in that "I don't care about money, prestige, power, or happiness" art school kind of way.

The Nest

Banking has its own Hens—Human Resources (HR) and assistants.

HR chicks, who, in some cleverly devised Banker pun, represent most of a Bank's "talent," actually recruit and help hire new talent. They're generally well put together, friendly, and chipper young women. They don't deal with money; rather, they manage "human capital," interviewing and courting new Bankers into the firm.*

Assistants are generally unattractive older women, but I met a cute, young one once, and the buzz I've generated around her has made her peers seem more intriguing. Expec-

---

* There are a few males in HR. Do not let them manage your human capital.

tations for this position include: absorbing verbal abuse, incorrectly scheduling appointments, and failing to not say something stupid when answering the phone.

A couple times a year, there will be a firm-wide event where the Back Office and the Front Office will socialize together. The dynamic is undoubtedly weird. It feels wrong, like a financial model with gross profit margin greater than 100 percent. In this case, a first-year Analyst didn't accidentally add revenues and costs, but we are still mistakenly forced together.

The Hens, however, are able to capitalize on these situations, as they're the closest thing to a real woman one can find within a Bank. They still possess that fresh, woman scent that female Bankers lose after their first fifteen minutes at work, and they leverage this to flirt with any and all Bankers. Hens don't particularly envy or despise Bankers; instead, they've opted to try to sleep with them.

Law Review

All Banks have their own in-house legal teams whose role is primarily to deal with compliance and other issues related directly to the Bank. Even more Back Officey, however, are the corporate law firms that Banks hire to conduct the legal diligence and transactional gruntwork for deals. Banks have allowed these law firms to create their own little companies and have gone as far as to help propagate an air of exclusivity within the group (some even call themselves "Big Law" firms). This is really all just smoke and mirrors to keep the poor lawyers quiet and writing memos while first-year Banking Analysts scream at them for not knowing how to multiply single-digit numbers or use the correct typeface. Transactional law does need to occur for a deal to go through, but in the scheme of things, they're not the product, they're quality assurance.

The saddest part about corporate lawyers, who I collectively and individually refer to as "Matlock," is that they generally work just as many hours as the Bankers they support, but they get compensated far less.

Lawyers use the phrase *term of art* when referring to a subject specific term or legalese. Bankers have our own "term of art" for lawyers: retarded.

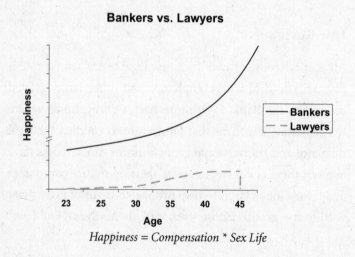

*Happiness = Compensation * Sex Life*

The Clearing(whore)house

I borrowed this vulgar moniker from my roommate Jon who, as a Trader, has had to deal with them. Clearinghouses also have a slightly more favorable name: "custodians."

Apparently, Clearinghouses are third parties or internal groups that ensure that the trades that Banks or Hedge Funds execute reconcile with what actually processes in the market. Essentially, Clearingwhores are given a massive stack of papers, and their job is to make sure that the two sets of numbers on them are identical. Page after page, they just keep going, making sure there are no discrepancies.

Sometimes, when Jon and I are bored, we'll play "Clearinghouse." The game consists of one of us making two columns of identical numbers, and the other pretending to figure out whether they're the same or not. I hit Jon with a particularly difficult one the other day:

1	1
1	1
1	1
1	1

He played the part of the Clearingwhore to a tee, mulling it over for an hour, scratching his head, perplexed, and then finally giving up. For the Clearingwhores reading—they are indeed the same. Write that down.

One would think that this process could get automated, which only reinforces the popular conception that Banks are kind, philanthropic entities concerned with maintaining America's domestic workforce.

I asked a Trader friend if he'd ever talked to someone at a Clearinghouse. He said that he had. "What did you say to him?" I asked. He told me he spoke a total of eight words: "I make the money. You just count it."

IT

> *"You fucking stupid Banker guy. I went to IIT Ahmedabad and got my master's degree in Computer Engineering and now this is what I am doing! I am ten thousand times smarter than you. You are eating my head, mule! American Dream and my foot! Jersey City sucks worse than the ghettos of Bihar. Just wait until I get into the Business Side of Banking, sister-fucker. Then you'll see!"*

That's what the online translator gave me when I sent in a recording of what my IT guy was muttering under his breath while reinstalling Windows on my computer.

American Dream? I believe that would be me.

$$\$ \$ \$$$

I suspect the Back Office is even bigger than I realize. I met a guy once who was a runner, for example, and his job was to run around on the Trading floor physically delivering orders (he even *wore* runners!). And most of what is technically the Middle Office (Risk Management, Compliance) could probably also be called the Back Office.

It may exist under a massive Banker shadow, but there are numerous benefits to working in the Back Office. They get Front Office–quality health and dental and a higher salary than anyone in their respective jobs at other places. Secretaries rip six figures consistently on good years. Most important, of course, Back Office Bankers have that indescribable pleasure of getting to tell people that they "work on Wall Street," which must still feel amazing, even if delivered unconvincingly.

COMMENTS FROM leveragedsellout.com

First of all, whenever someone in HR starts saying things like "divide," you should probably stop listening to them.

POSTED BY MONKEY, NOV 16, 12:40 P.M.

Has it occurred to you that you are every bit the bitch for carlysle that the schoolteachers are to you? You can fake it, kid, but you are still just a wannabe with an expense account.

POSTED BY ROGER, JULY 30, 4:24 P.M.

I think we all know that Roger is the biggest rainmaker in the Compliance department at Wells Fargo Securities.

POSTED BY ANONYMOUS, JULY 30, 5:24 P.M.

All comments are real and unedited.

CASE STUDY: THE STATE SCHOOLER

This comes from Alex, a Penn State student whose experience speaks for all his XYU/XSU Banking brethren.

Yeah, no kidding—it's pretty tough being a state school kid in Banking. When people at work ask me where I went to school, I can literally see their eyes go blank when I say the word *State*—it's like I've uttered a racial slur or said something so appalling that the only way their brains can handle it is to substitute my voice with white noise. As their eyes refocus, they'll usually ask, "Oh . . . UPenn?" I'll lower my head and tell them, "No . . . Penn State." And then, fantastically uncomfortable, they'll eke out something like: "Oh, wow. Musta been a really fun experience . . . great football team." We'll linger for a moment in an awkward pause, and then I officially cease to exist to them.

It wasn't easy getting to where I am today. I took a ton of finance classes in undergrad to prove my dedication to the field, and when I started my job at a Bulge-Bracket Investment Bank (which was a reach), I thought that the coursework we did would give me an added edge. I figured I'd be a super-Banker of sorts, bursting out of the gates and impressing everyone with my tangible, value-add skills. And I did, I really did! For a moment, the State School kid knew more than everyone! But, sadly, this lasted only three days before those smartass Princeton and Harvard guys mastered everything it had taken me four years to learn. Argh! Dudes were better than me by week two.

You see, in Banking, your school is one of those things that boosts you up or, in my case, haunts you for the rest of your life. I'll never forget trying to interview at Hedge Funds. During a final-round interview, a forty-five-year-old, accomplished man in finance welcomed me into his regal office, and we sat down. He pulled my résumé from his file and looked it over. I could see him do a double-take when he saw Penn State University written in bold letters. It didn't matter that it had Honors Program, 4.0/4.0 GPA, and Phi Beta Kappa written underneath it, he seemed genuinely perplexed.

He turned the paper over, as if the name of a better school might be written on the back. Then he shook it; maybe the whole sheet would turn blank like an Etch A Sketch, and we could start again from scratch. It didn't. Unsatisfied, he furrowed his brow, looked at me apologetically, and said, candidly, "I'm sorry, I don't interview for the administrative positions."

Story of my motherfucking life.

PERFORMANCE REVIEW #2

1. A Williams College alumnus is spotted on Wall Street. His occupation is a six-letter word starting with *B* and ending with *R*. What is he?

   The correct answer: beggar.

2. A Banker Girl will tell you she is going to switch careers and move into fashion.
   a. Sometimes
   b. Always
   c. Never

   The correct answer: b.

3. Wall Street _____ diversity.
   a. scowls at
   b. does not know the definition of
   c. embraces
   d. fakes
   e. mocks

   The correct answer: c.

4. You receive an e-mail from a headhunter. You:
   a. Respond
   b. Delete
   c. Report Spam

   The correct answer: c.

5. Andy, Jeff, Paulos, Shane, Samir, and Rex are all Big Lawyers. There are exactly six chairs evenly spaced around a circular table. The chairs are numbered 1 through 6, with successively numbered chairs next to each other and chair 1 next to chair 6. Each chair is occupied by exactly one of the Big Lawyers. The following conditions apply:

> Rex sits immediately next to Shane.
> Jeff sits immediately next to Paulos, Shane, or both.
> Andy does not sit immediately next to Paulos.
> If Samir sits immediately next to Rex, Samir does not sit immediately next to Paulos.

Which one of the following seating arrangements of the six Big Lawyers in chairs 1 through 6 would *not* violate the stated conditions?

a. Andy, Rex, Shane, Paulos, Samir, Jeff

b. Andy, Jeff, Paulos, Samir, Rex, Shane

c. Andy, Samir, Rex, Shane, Jeff, Paulos

d. Andy, Shane, Jeff, Samir, Paulos, Rex

e. Douchebag, douchebag, douchebag, douchebag, douchebag, douchebag

The correct answer: e.

Culture

FACT #10

Even this T-shirt
is bespoke.
Fashion

FASHION IS A MEANS of personal expression. Clothes broadcast emotion and can speak volumes about one's inner character. People send out different cues about their nature with their outfits: self-confidence, conformity, reckless individuality. As Bankers, we, too, utilize fashion for personal communication, and the singular message our finely woven threads scream is an unrelenting: "We are better than you."

$$\$ \ \$ \ \$$

On a Saturday morning, I call up my friend Hugh, twice, getting him on the second attempt. I wake him from what I know is a deep, post-drunk sleep.

"What the fuck?" he answers groggily, possibly speaking into the wrong end of the phone.

"It's ten thirty a.m.," I inform him. Then, coolly: "And I just spent six hundred bucks."

He turns in his bed, grunts, and responds: "Who cares?"

Hugh doesn't quite *get* it. I elaborate: "On *socks,* man! On socks!

"No one even sees those," I explain, pausing and waiting for the explanation to sink in. Then I brush my knuckles against my blazer and proclaim my title: "I really am the MBP."

I hear an exasperated arm slam against his mattress, and he yells: "What the hell are you talking about right now?"

Even though he should already know, I define it for him: "The Most Ballingest Player, kid. The Most Ballingest Player." And I hang up.

$$\$ \$ \$$$

The $600 is only the beginning, and I continue shopping, making my way from store to store to replenish my perfect Banker wardrobe. At first, spending a bunch of cash sounded like a fun exercise, but by noon, the MBP is officially pissed off.

I've already been to six places, and I still have to pick up a couple suits from Armani. In a cab in Midtown Manhattan, stuck in gridlocked traffic, my frustration explodes upon the driver: "Step on it!" I scream.

I really don't have time for this kind of shit, I think, remembering a pile of analysis I still have to do before Monday. I need a personal shopper, an assistant, or a girlfriend—someone who can just buy me a bunch of shit and throw away whatever I don't like.

I mentally craft the business plan for a one-stop Banker clothing store that would solve all these problems: it would

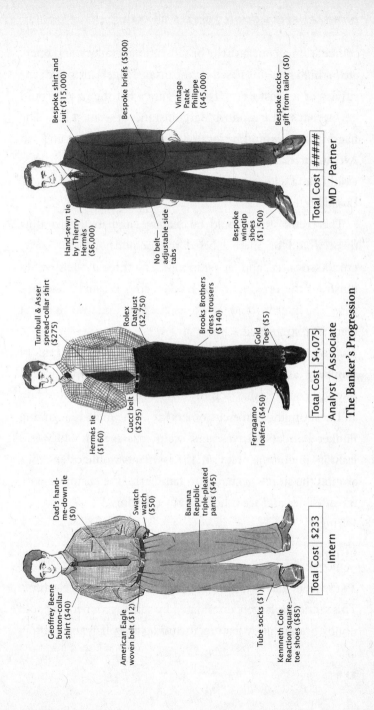

The Banker's Progression

Intern

Total Cost $233

- Dad's hand-me-down tie ($0)
- Swatch watch ($50)
- Banana Republic triple-pleated pants ($45)
- Geoffrey Beene button-collar shirt ($40)
- American Eagle woven belt ($12)
- Tube socks ($1)
- Kenneth Cole Reaction square-toe shoes ($85)

Analyst / Associate

Total Cost $4,075

- Turnbull & Asser spread-collar shirt ($275)
- Rolex Datejust ($2,750)
- Brooks Brothers dress trousers ($140)
- Hermès tie ($160)
- Gucci belt ($295)
- Gold Toes ($5)
- Ferragamo loafers ($450)

MD / Partner

Total Cost ####

- Bespoke shirt and suit ($15,000)
- Bespoke briefs ($500)
- Vintage Patek Philippe ($45,000)
- Bespoke socks—gift from tailor ($0)
- Hand-sewn tie by Thierry Hermès ($6,000)
- No belt—adjustable side tabs
- Bespoke wingtip shoes ($1,500)

source from all our favorite brands, employ tailors, and operate on high margins based on the insanely inelastic price sensitivity of its customers. I'm not sure what the name would be, perhaps Morgandorf Bergoldstone or something. The flagship store would be located at Fifty-ninth Street and 5th Avenue across the street from the Apple Store, and there would be a satellite store in the Financial District, at 87 Broad Street.

The men's store would be massive, and in the window there would be three labeled mannequins: INTERN, ANALYST/ASSOCIATE, and MD/PARTNER. The three models would illustrate the progression a Banker goes through, fashionwise. The intern would have a special note underneath it that read: NOT SOLD HERE.

Morgandorf Bergoldstone would have the perfect kind of shopping assistants: hot, foreign, and liberal with casual physical contact. Also, scantily clad. Generally, they would do all the shopping while customers sat at the man-spa, getting Banker haircuts, shaves, and scalp massages in old-world fashion. But on the first visit, the assistants would offer a tour around the store—a chance to familiarize the customer with the offerings and see if he "has any questions."

Shirts

To the front and left, there's an area for off-the-rack clothing. This section is largely dominated by shirts, grouped and sold not by brand but by feature, including fit, collar, and cuff.

Fit

Historically, Banker shirts have been huge sails that fit like garbage bags, loose and billowy. Slimmer fitted shirts, however, are now in favor and widely available in the store. While it may look silly, the baggy shirt is still for purchase. It's a tribute to Banker history, and some actually still prefer it, especially when the elevator is busy and Bankers can untuck their parachute-like shirts, catch the breeze, and coast safely to the ground floor.

Collar

Shirts are further matrixed by collar type. They are labeled "BACK OFFICE," "MIDDLE OFFICE," and "FRONT OFFICE," corresponding to button, standard, and spread collar.

At my desk, we once had this Iranian kid intern who wore a button-collar shirt his first day to work. Naturally, we nicknamed him Buttons. He was mortified, and in response made the mistake of telling us that his father wore short-sleeved collared shirts to work, so he really had no point of reference. Then, despite his skin tone, we just started calling him White Trash.

Banker ties are kept near the shirts and knotted appropriately with respective collars to illustrate that a spread-collar shirt is naked with only a half Windsor, and a narrow-collar shirt with a thick, full Windsor just feels off-beam, like putting twenty-two-inch rims on a Prius. Hermès, Ferragamo, and their peers dominate this section.

Cuffs

Cuffs are an often overlooked feature of the shirt, but not at Morgandorf Bergoldstone. I'm not sure where standard cuffs are acceptable, but here, they are substandard.

I once worked on a deal that required me to go to the Paris office. After seeing them get hammered on wine at lunch and comply with regulated thirty-six-hour work weeks, I can safely say that French cuffs are the most significant contribution the French have made to Banking, beating out the Bank BNP Paribas by a wide margin.

Double-button barrel cuffs are the next step up.

The store offers monogramming services for cuffs and breast pockets, but only in certain situations, as it can come off tacky and smack of L.L. Bean backpacks.

The other half of the store is dedicated to custom-tailored clothing. All the world's finest tailors work at Morgandorf Bergoldstone, and, in heavy accents, they lecture customers on the difference between true bespoke clothing (made from scratch) and made-to-measure (adapted from an existing pattern). Bankers laugh and joke with the tailors that, unlike clothes, a "made-to-measure" woman is sometimes ideal, fitting perfectly after a variety of nips, tucks, and subtle insults.

The tailors create custom shirts, but mainly focus on bespoke suits.

Suits

Everyone dresses in a suit at some point. Whether it's that special business meeting, a funeral, or a family wedding, the average man puts on something resembling a suit every once in a while. I imagine that in these moments, this otherwise regular man must feel empowered and confident. His posture improved and his gait quickened, he will, for a moment, live life with the confidence and stature of a real man. Then there will be a strong breeze, and his piece-of-shit suit will dissolve in the wind, leaving him naked and, once again, painfully average.

Our Banker Suits are navy, gray, or black with thin pinstripes or other subtle patterns. They are made from fine Italian cloth and stitched with life-or-death thoroughness, because unlike a Joe who *dresses in* suits occasionally, Bankers *wear* suits frequently.

Actually, the regularity with which a Banker wears a suit varies by age, rank, and Bank policy, and in the modern era, many Banks have switched from business formal to business casual. Dressing in a suit daily to a Bank that is business casual is overeager and a telltale sign of a gunner. Sell Side Bankers tend to go formal more frequently than the Buy Side, but whatever the case, every Banker needs several good suits, and Morgandorf Bergoldstone provides the solution.

In the fitting area, there is a monstrous fifty-foot magnifying mirror. Bankers stand in front of it, launching M&A lasers out of their elbows and inspecting themselves in their new threads. Here, they get a brief glimpse into how society regularly sees them: larger than life.

$$\$ \ \$ \ \$$$

I snap out of my reverie, and back in the cab, we've moved approximately five feet. And that was only to box out a pedestrian. I consider getting out and walking, but that would require, well, walking. Instead, I roll my thumb over my Black-Berry wheel restlessly and mentally browse my packed Outlook calendar. I inspect the people walking by on the sidewalk.

I see a tall, dark-haired model type in long leather boots and jeans. She passes, talking on her phone, and I consider balling up my business card and chucking it at her. My aim is pretty good, and if she unfolds it, that's a guaranteed close.

A thirty-something man who looks like an advertising exec walks by in a loud, obnoxious blue suit with huge pin-stripes. "Wannabe MBP," I mutter, imagining him working in a mail room to "get his start."

The cab inches forward, and I see that in the taxi next to me, there's another restless guy in a pink, popped-collar polo.

Banker? I tilt my head and think.

Beach and Casual Wear

Morgandorf Bergoldstone also has a robust Banker Beach and Casual Wear section, and it's overwhelmingly pastel to

keep us looking "sweet." Polos, shorts, pants—
they're all Nantucket Red, Jake Blue, or Bermuda
Pink. From J.McLaughlin, Vineyard Vines, and
other stores, the fabrics are poplin, madras,
and seersucker, and the belts are not leather,
they're cloth and D-ringed. Like in the formal section, ties are silk, but now they are
patterned with sailboats, airplanes, whales,
dolphins, and other things that remind Bankers
what they should buy, ride, and hunt.

Accessories

Immediately next to the Beach and Casual section are accessories. Rolex, IWC, and various
other watches are displayed freely (there's no
need for protective glass). The watches here,
however, are subtle in their ostentation—they're not the size
of saucers, and they cannot give precise nautical bearings.
There are some pocket handkerchiefs, no tiepins, and a wide
selection of silk knots and cuff links.

Shoes

Directly in the middle of the store are all the Banker Shoes.
Just like in my closet, Rainbow Sandals and Gray Newbies
coexist with Ferragamo loafers and cap- and straight-toe

shoes. Wingtips are off to the side, for the slightly older Bankers.

Loafers are the centerpiece of the exhibit, as they're the consummate Banker shoe. They're versatile—they can almost always be worn to the office, and you can sport them with or without socks, paired with shorts, and even to bed to let a girl know you really mean business.

I, personally, like my loafers like I like my women: expensive, fit, and, more often than not, with a bit of bling around their necks. Loafers with gold links catch the light occasionally, like when one crosses his legs. Getting a glimpse of them is like spotting an undercover officer's concealed weapon and coming to the realization that someone you thought was an innocuous human being is actually equipped to fuck you up. A dude in Tod's loafers, however, is probably more lethal than any law enforcement agent.

If Gucci or Prada made women the quality of their loafers, I'd probably have a closetful, and I'd rock them just like I do my loafers: bareback.

Banker Chick Clothing

It should be noted that Morgandorf Bergoldstone does have a woman's store for female Bankers, but it's not across the street as you might expect; it's located a few blocks away in the basement of an H&M. While real women are meant to wear bright clothes that accentuate their figures and expose skin, Banker Girls must be strictly prohibited from this practice. As such, the women's store sells only bland colors from the likes of BCBG, Theory, and I don't know who else. A handful of pashmina shawls and innovative hair devices are also sold for the few girls looking to spice things up.

Banker Girls repeatedly request that the store stock red-soled Christian Louboutins, which are subtle yet powerful, like loafer links, but the designer absolutely refuses, claiming it would "destroy his brand."

Banana Republic and Ann Taylor, on the other hand, eagerly sign up.

My cabbie is finally able to wade through the traffic, and we make it to the Armani store.

I enter, and the door is held for me by a middle-aged married couple in front of me. They're achingly tourist, in "I ❤ New York" hats, fanny packs, and exposed cameras. I shake my head, step back, and let them go in without me.

I reflect on the most important feature laid out in Morgandorf Bergoldstone's business plan: the application process. To shop at the store, potential customers must be filtered just as rigorously as applicants are when they try to get a job in finance.

Employment histories are researched for Wall Street pedigree, and a set of in-depth interviews, both fit and technical, are conducted to weed out the rabble. The process is somewhat cumbersome but ensures that what just happened to me at Armani never, ever occurs again.

Word of the store would disseminate quickly, of course, and soon Hollywood celebrities and international industrialists would be trying furiously to be granted acceptance. Rock stars would all of a sudden befriend Bankers at clubs, begging them to "pull some strings" to make up for their poor GPAs.

Jay-Z might even approach my table at a restaurant. A poor man's MBP, he'd be wearing a jet black tuxedo with a white scarf and aviator sunglasses. Yankees hat in hand, he'd speak in an awkward attempt at professionalism, subtly letting me know that he's going to be "shooting over" his application to Morgandorf Bergoldstone. He just wanted to "reach out."

I don't stop eating, but I consider him briefly as a candidate: worth about $550 million, the CEO of two major record labels, co-owner of the New Jersey Nets.

"Should I 'rally the troops'?" I think. "Is ol' Jigga worth my 'banging the table'?"

I come to a decision and do what I do whenever I get this question from some eager Third-Tier college student. I shrug my shoulders in a fake apology and respond, addressing him by his first name to ease the blow, slightly.

"Sorry, Shawn," I offer with translucent empathy. "We just don't have that many positions opening up right now."

COMMENTS FROM leveragedsellout.com

There really were different standards on the street a few years ago. People got sent HOME for wearing the wrong thing. A former boss of mine who got his first gig with Jim Rogers loved to tell the story of going to lunch with him wearing brown loafers with tassels. "No!" shouted Jim, pointing at his feet. "F! That is an F!!!"

POSTED BY EV, DEC 12, 4:24 P.M.

All comments are real and unedited.

FACT #11

It's all about the bonuses, baby.

Compensation

'M NOT SURE how many e-mail forwards I receive over the course of a year. Hundreds? Thousands? They range from anecdotes of stupid Bankers exposing themselves to the media to bitter "I hate my life. I quit" departure manifestos to revealing pictures of the girls my colleagues have slept with, and, much like the girls themselves, the forwards vary in appeal.

I still remember the best e-mail forward I've ever gotten; it came during the early summer months of my first year as an Analyst. I personally hadn't lost my perspective on Banking, but the endless hours of toil and diligence had been wearing on others. When this note made its way around The Street, however, everyone surged with pride. It reiterated to us why finance is not only the sport of champions, it is truly The Greatest Profession on Earth. The e-mail carried an attachment, and the file name was: Analyst Bonus Numbers— 2006.xls.

The file, in Excel format, of course, detailed the projected

Bonus figures for the year. In one column, each major Bank name was listed. Next to these names, a dollar value for each first-year, second-year, and third-year Analyst was given. Every Bank's number was verified by a trusted "Source," which ranged from "Citi Staffer" to "MS Analyst" to "Rumor."

Everyone I know got that e-mail, and while the Bonus amounts differed based on Bank performance and prestige, it really didn't matter. All the numbers were huge.

An e-mail like this comes around every year (the numbers were even bigger in 2007), and it's testament to the fact that our employers truly care about us. While other corporations might treat their employees like drones they can "burn and churn," Investment Banks *nurture*. Through various forms of compensation, we're cultivated, supported, and rewarded for our efforts.

BlackBerries

Tons of randoms have BlackBerries these days, but it is and always will be a Banker tool. Modern-day katana swords, they are marks of our caste that we treat with the same level of respect as did our Samurai counterparts. Ancient warriors slept with their swords under their pillows, took great care to maintain them, and, ultimately, used them in battle. Bankers' BlackBerries are equally lethal, but they're plastic and have somewhat more Anglo-Saxon names.

Every Banker is given a BlackBerry, which he is meant to

keep on his person at all times. Often, younger Bankers will receive older models to separate them from their superiors and give them something to work toward. In all cases, however, these devices are intended to ensure real-time messaging and accessibility. A BlackBerry must be both on and within reach so that even if it is "out of pocket," the Banker it belongs to never is. Some

Peter and his BlackBerry, Peter

consider BlackBerries to be excessively tethering, causing work to encroach on private life. I don't really follow the logic.

Perhaps the most rewarding aspect of BlackBerries is the built-in game BrickBreaker. The premise of the game is simple: move a paddle to destroy targets and accumulate points—not very different from Banking, where we're taking down deals and trades and aggregating sums of cash. The game is played everywhere: on calls, during in-person meets, and in the bathroom. In a stressful life, it's a calming, cathartic experience.

The only time you might see our BlackBerries powered off is on an airplane. Actually, that wouldn't happen—you fly commercial.

Black Cars

Back in my early days, a ride home in a black car was a prize. While a Lincoln Town Car might not be anything extraordinary, it represents the exclusivity that we Bankers cherish.

I *earned* the vouchers that got me into those cars. Working late didn't seem so bad when I had a comfortable ride home to look forward to; even waiting in a long line of colleagues in subzero temperatures to get a car while dozens of taxis whipped by me seemed natural. Commoners ride yellow; Bankers ride black.

Being inside a black car was a sanctuary, a well-deserved lordship. I relished treating the driver like my personal bitch, and even more so, I relished looking out the window at everyone else "walking," or "taking the subway."

I start in PE next year, and I'm not certain what kind of hitter chariot my PE firm will arrange to take me home at night. But one thing's for certain: it will be black and appropriately Top-Tier.

Meals

I usually either expense meals at a nearby restaurant or my food comes directly to the office via SeamlessWeb, a Web site that facilitates expensing meals at work. It's a great utility but must be used carefully.

An Analyst in my group, Caroline, came into Banking with the build of a thin, ex–tennis player, but she immediately became obsessed with SeamlessWeb. Within weeks, she was patting her burgeoning stomach as she clicked around the Web site, salivating over what she might order. She had developed what we refer to in the industry as "SeamlessWeb Belly."

Caroline and others like her have created a well-defined science built around meal expensing. Most Banks have a set amount that can be spent per individual and, though we're not cheap, there's an analytical appeal to maximizing the food one can purchase. We'll throw in an extra bag of chips or an extraneous Red Bull, just to get as close to the limit as possible. Some Bankers will even apply this strategy at delis, where they'll try to expense away their household shopping. I heard of a guy at Morgan Stanley who bought razors on the firm but was caught red-handed when he was required to provide an itemized receipt.*

Out of the office, Bankers eat steak dinners. Whatever the occasion—perhaps we've finished up a deal, hired or fired someone, or perhaps it's just a regular Tuesday—we'll eat steak. High-end steakhouses generate upward of 90 percent of their revenue from Bankers, where bottles of fine wine are paired with fine meat and what our waiter might incorrectly pronounce as "*fine*-ance conversation." Spearing a prime slab of flesh reminds me that if we Bankers weren't tearing down M&A deals and buyouts, we'd be out hunting boar, bucks, or other big game.

---

*Traders are voracious, eat all the time, and graze throughout the day on free candy sent to them by the New York Stock Exchange. They do not use SeamlessWeb, because McDonald's and Quiznos are not yet a part of the system.

133

Bonuses

Bonuses are the biggest part of Banker compensation. They tend to vary year to year based on the market, but even in bad years they're still enough to open doors, upgrade yachts, and put you in a special Banker tax bracket.

In Investment Banking, Analysts are grouped into tiers based on reviews. Last year I was Top Tier, meaning that I was the best, and so I got the largest payout of our group's bonus pool. For others, bonus size is often directly driven by how much money they bring into the firm.

No matter how you rank in your firm, Bonus season is the best part of the Banker calendar. Falling in the summer for Analysts and during the winter for others, it's a time that retail businesses have to build into their accounting methods and one that compels regular guys to dress up and try to pass themselves off as Bankers. Girls are acutely aware of Bonus season, and, like a Gucci bag purchased from a streetside vendor, they can sniff out these fakes from a mile away.

I know a first-year Analyst who told everyone he was going to "lever up" his Bonus and buy a place in the Hamptons. Other guys purchase Porsches that they park in a garage and get to drive a couple times a year. Both are rational investments, but I prefer to take a significant percentage of my Bonus and throw an elaborate Bonus party where, in the company of some beautiful females, my friends and I can celebrate the rewards of The Greatest Profession on Earth.

INVESTMENT BANKING ANALYST TIERING

In Investment Banking, Analysts are divided into tiers that dictate compensation. *Top Tier* is the phrase that every young Banker fantasizes about. Even saying the word *bottom* in their presence will cause them to stick their fingers in their ears and scream, blocking out any potential *tier* that may follow, jinx them, and doom them to poverty.

Top Tier: Mark, the ambitious young Banker with an uncanny sense of numbers, gets the largest payout. Valuation is seemingly instinctual to him and a company's financials are puzzle pieces he strings together to create beautiful works of art. He is polished, appropriate, and charming, and able to heighten and throttle these attributes when necessary.

Second Tier: Susan. Like her, her Bonus is decent. Extremely diligent, works well with others, and shares her knowledge when appropriate. Knows when to speak up and when to be quiet, but lacks that bit of "something special" that separates her from the Top Tier. It is obvious that she has been battling this same issue her entire life, and she acquiesces to her fate. She might perform at a higher level if someone encouraged her and gave her the opportunity, but no Bank is willing to take that risk.

Third Tier: Jason. Receives a paltry Bonus (by Banking standards). Is perpetually nervous and takes short breaks from hyperventilating only to bite his nails. Cannot be taken to meetings or trusted to "take ownership" of anything. Socks occasionally clash with shoes. Also, Amir. Does blow in the bathroom and speaks at length about his passion for DJing house music.

Bottom Tier: The dude that just got fired, left crying, and had to be chased after by security to repossess his BlackBerry, whose screen reads GAME OVER.

COMMENTS FROM leveragedsellout.com

My current score is 57,897,175 and I have 4,516 lives left. I hope I don't die anytime soon because I haven't eaten or drunk anything or even slept for nineteen days straight. In case I do die while doing this, does someone want to continue my game on my BlackBerry for me? Who's down? The handoff might be a bit tricky since I would like to play until my last breath . . .

My MD can't even look me in the eyes when he talks to me anymore . . .

POSTED BY GOD, FEB 22, 5:44 P.M.

All comments are real and unedited.

FACT #12

It's all Jersey to me.
Geography

NEW YORK IS the only true Banker city. It's where all the magic happens.

Other cities revolve around their own puny industries, but in Manhattan, finance is center stage; the residents are either humbly serving us or trying feverishly to get in on a piece of the action. Bankers own all the best real estate and run the most exclusive private clubs. We are the lifeblood of the city, dictating trends and serving as the hub for all major social gatherings.

"Wall Street" and "Midtown" are not concepts here; they are physical places where the presence of Bankers is truly palpable. For residences, we primarily choose the prestigious: the Hill (Murray Hill), the Buy Side (Upper East Side), FiDi (Financial District), and a few other select downtown neighborhoods we deem worthy of gentrification. For older financiers, Westchester, New York, and the nicer areas of Connecticut offer comfortable Banker suburbs where children may play safely in the streets.

The World of Banking

Offices outside of New York are commonly known as "regional" or "satellite" or "insignificant." While they may claim to maintain the "Wall Street state of mind," they never quite get it. I've been to every major city in the world, and I can safely say that New York is the National Banking Champion of the past forever years, and everywhere else is just JV.

While traveling to these boondocks, I can't help but feel like a transplanted all-state quarterback among uncoordinated rejects. I'm casually running in touchdowns all by myself while both the other team and my own receivers are fumbling about, clueless.

London

Of the JV squad, London's game is the most promising. It has decent fundamentals and seems to understand the basic concepts, but it's just not quite there.

London is the B-list celeb version of Manhattan; it's the Freddy Prinze Jr. to our Leonardo DiCaprio. It's island-ish, which is good, and when visiting, I've noticed they even have their own B&T (bridge and tunnel) crowd, the "chavs," who are just as annoying and omnipresent as our own. An Essex girl has the same slum-appeal as our Long Island and Jersey chicks, and they're just as eager to meet Bankers.

Our friends "across the pond" are gaining steam based on the growing European market, but while it may have been the foundation for men's tailoring, London will never be the epicenter of Banking. The names aren't even right. The Square Mile and Canary Wharf are poor-man's versions of our Financial District. "CanWhar?" "TheSquaMi?" Those don't sound anywhere near as cool as "FiDi." And neither does "Investment *Wanker.*"

Bankers starting out in London will always be sent to New York for training, not the other way around (you don't count, Barclays!). There are no blockbuster British companies looking to IPO, and the only big PE shop over there recognizes its uniqueness in London; the firm Permira claims its name translates to "very special, very different." The most famous British Bank, N. M. Rothschild & Sons, carried some clout in the 1800s, but that family is now more focused on wine-making.

In the long run, London will do quite well for itself, like a TV actor who has the occasional breakout supporting character role, but, despite its best efforts, it will just never be in the spotlight. Different? Yes. Special? No.

San Francisco

San Francisco is another half-decent junior varsity player, but she plays in a weird, Ultimate Frisbee–ish manner.

San Fran probably has the second largest population of Bankers in the United States, and they live in places like the Marina and Pacific Heights and wander around their city with the ever-present fear that their girlfriends might jump ship for some billionaire start-up geek.

Even speaking on the phone with SF Bankers is troubling. You'll be trying to conduct business, and then they'll say something like: "Yo bro, this model I made is hella sick" or "My bonus is gonna be hecka big, kid!" What kinds of adverbs are those?

Thankfully, you're allowed to say, "Yo! You're hella regional!" and hang up on them immediately.

Chicago

I had a friend who worked in the Chicago office of a large Investment Bank, and one time, after several rounds, he leaked the fact that he was forced to bind his own pitch books and had to physically call to order dinner because only the New York office had a production department and SeamlessWeb. How lame is that?

As a player on the JV squad, Chicago is the terrible kicker, doubling up his mini JV soccer letter with another one in football. He misses twenty-five-yard field goals, and if New York scores a touchdown, Chicago will screw up the extra point.

While Chicago may be known as the Second (Tier) City, it is really the Twelfth (Tier) Banking City, despite a couple large Hedge Funds out there. The only impressive thing about it is that it successfully manages to be the polar opposite of Manhattan. Unlike our elite country club, Chicago is a collection of meathead frat dudes and hicks going ga-ga, stuffing their faces with hot dogs at Wiener Circle.

Young Bankers in Chicago tend to live in Lincoln Park, moving on to the Gold Coast and eventually North Shore areas. Chicago's mediocrity is a prime example of the degeneration that occurs when you can rent a decent-sized apartment for only $400 per month, so no one should ever, ever bitch about Manhattan's high rent prices—the sifting is necessary.

In terms of nightlife, Chicago makes an almost charmingly pathetic effort at having "hip" lounges and clubs that cater to wealthy young professionals. The Chicagoans just can't seem to pull it together, though, and asking for "bottle service" will probably leave you at a table with a bucket of seven-ounce pony beers, several faded sorority sisters, and a free round of Jell-O shots.

Los Angeles

LA Bankers are generally out in the middle of the football field, wide open and waving their hands above their heads eagerly in hopes of getting passed the ball. This is never indulged, but I will occasionally toss a pump-fake their direction, just so someone comes and tackles the shit out of them.

A lot of West Coast Bankers have a not-so-extraordinary dream of starting their own fund and being able to run it from a beachfront property in San Diego, surfing and exploring "nature." Until they reach this misguided pinnacle, they're generally stuck in the wasteland that is Los Angeles.

It seems that in LA, people tend to value working in Hollywood more than working in finance. I tip my hat to those in that industry for creating their own little personal fantasy land and cede to them all their plastic-surgery-ridden bleached blondes; Bankers have a stronghold on the rest of the world.

Note to Bankers in LA—get the fuck out.

Asia

The JV Banking team has a waterboy, an Asian kid everyone refers to as "Asia." He provides replenishment, but it comes in the form of his women, and he's never allowed to drink the Gatorade he dispenses.

Asian women in Asia are, remarkably, even more attracted to Bankers than Asian women in America. As such, being a good-looking white man in Asia is being part of a successful sex oligopoly. There are few of us and there is insane demand, and this is why Banking in Asia is awesome. Everyone from schoolgirls in Tokyo to Hong Kong socialites will physically throw themselves at those in finance, doing anything to win our praise and conversation.

Asian girls even trick Bankers into sleeping with them under the guise of practicing English or brushing up on finance concepts. "Rye-boar!" they'll scream, and the London Interbank Offered Rate (LIBOR) will have never seemed more confusing.

Even Banker Chicks will feel wanted for once in Asia, as the natives will pet their blond hair in fascination and mimic their arrhythmic dance moves. No market with Bankers is perfect, but in Asia our product is much more overtly and aggressively sought after than anywhere else.

Beyond this, Asia is unimportant. There appear to be some signs of economic development and growth of the Private Equity business in China, perhaps added bonuses to the existing privileged status we hold.

There are, of course, other satellite cities—the Little League perhaps. As for the JV squad, I will admit I do occasionally enjoy traveling out to visit, dominate, and inspire their awe. But ultimately, there's nothing like coming home and playing in New York, in front of millions of my fans.

INSIDER INFO WITH HANNAH

I'm a San Fran girl, born and raised. And despite what people may assume, I'm not some hemp necklace–wearing, bong-smoking hippie chick from Berkeley. No, I'm an attractive young female from a good family in Atherton, and I played both lacrosse and tennis in high school.

The other night, I had to make quite a decision, and the Silicon Valley dynamic came into play. I was out at a bar with my friends, and before I knew it, I was talking to two guys, both attractive, one who worked for Google and one who worked at Goldman Sachs.

I had to choose between the two, and even though I knew they were both rich, they couldn't have been more different. The Goldman guy, Hank, had on a crisp suit, Gucci loafers, and a Hublot. Sergei, the Googler, on the other hand, was wearing track pants, Birkenstocks, and a Timex. Hank bought me drink after drink while Sergei proposed we take turns buying rounds. And as for conversation, Sergei kept asking me questions about *me,* putting me on the spot to describe *my* interests and *my* "passions." Hank seemed quite content to just talk about himself.

They both had their pros and cons, but I knew for certain the competition was over after they both asked me out. Hank promised to drive me out to Napa in his *continued*

S4 convertible for dinner at French Laundry, and, um . . . Sergei told me he'd "take me to lunch at the Googleplex."

I don't care how nice that cafeteria is, Sergei, at least Bankers know how to treat a girl right!

COMMENTS FROM leveragedsellout.com

1. NYC during summer is one of the most disgusting places in the country. It's hot and humid, with millions of people cramped on a small island. Add to this the smell of garbage, and NYC in summer is nothing more than a hellhole. Chicago has Lake Michigan, which is an awesome place to jog and play sports.

2. The nightlife in Chicago is amazing. There's something going on every night. Stone Lotus, RiNo, the Underground, Manor, Enclave, Level, Y Bar, and Narcisse are just a few of the happening clubs and lounges. The girls there are some of the hottest you'll see in the country, but, of course, they don't go for fat NYC douche bags.

3. The energy here is incredible. Walk on Rush Street on a summer afternoon, and you'll know what I'm talking about. Awesome restaurants, shops, and beautiful women everywhere.

POSTED BY CHICAGO RULES, JUN 19, 1:48 P.M.
& NOV 13, 1:53 P.M.

Where is Chicago located exactly?

POSTED BY LSJU, SEP 11, 5:52 AM

Living large here in CAR (Central African Republic). Incredible women—kind of hard to communicate with them, though, b/c I have no French, and my Sango is pretty elementary.

Last week I traveled to Lagos (business class!) to pitch Avante Capital on the privatization of the Dzanga-Sangha National Park. Stayed at the Lagos Hilton!

No bottle service here in Bangui, but I bought a couple of bars with part of my last paycheck. I reserve the entire joint whenever I want to head out with the lads.

Then we get our crew to bring in a load of hot women. There are over eighty ethnic groups in CAR, so we mix it up to keep things interesting—Tuesday is Baya Ladies Night, Wednesday is Banda, and so on.

Personally, I think the M'Baka and Yakoma chicks are the hottest, but that's just me.

POSTED BY BALLER ANALYST IN BANGUI ON NOV 27, 1:55 PM

i'm out here drilling eskimo chicks on the north pole. pitching the russians on an uzi factory. i'm the coolest dude on the island, flying in grey goose for all the hos pimping it up cold as ice in my iglu.

POSTED BY BALLER ANALYST 2 ON NOV 29, 3:12 AM

All comments are real and unedited.

CASE STUDY: THE SHITSHOW

A friend relates a story of what happens to those who forget their places in life.

I work in Private Equity at DLJ Merchant Banking. You may be familiar with the name from *Monkey Business*—Credit Suisse was hip enough to pass the infamous title of its acquisition to its most elite group, and we make sure to rub it in everyone's faces. I've been there about a year, and it is pretty much living up to everything I've been dreaming about since I was a young chap in an overcoat, freezing in the cold New England winters at Deerfield. Anyway, whatever, forget about me.

The point here is somehow this guy landed a job here straight out of consulting. How bush league, right? What's next? Accountants, auditors, Chinese gold farmers? When I heard we were hiring someone from Bain (or maybe it was McKinsey or BCG—anyway, one of those "I couldn't get a job in finance" places), I thought, *Maybe he's pedigree? Maybe he's a Rockefeller?* But no, I checked my trusty pocket-sized Social Register, and his surname didn't appear anywhere. How curious.

I soon found out that this guy was more than just not pedigree. Josh (that's his name) was a skinny little Jewish dude from Jersey with a lisp. He had an awkwardly receding hairline and talked—stammered rather—like he was twelve, making up an excuse why his socks were always stuck together. Let's forget about the schmo's God-given features, get this—on his second day, Josh comes in to work at like 9:10, and he's rocking tan *khakis* and a long-sleeve polo. I swear I almost fell to the ground laughing when I saw those hideous pleated monstrosities and that shitty lint-infested, vertically disintegrated manufacturing-made shirt. What a doofus.

Bro, I know you made only like $55k traveling to Bumble-fuck, Idaho, every week to provide "strategic insight" and "thought leadership," but please, at least go to TJ Maxx and get some slightly imperfect Brooks Brothers. Get on eBay or something and buy that shit used for God's sakes. Yes, your mom and your broke-ass girlfriend both got you gift certificates to Banana for Christmas, but that doesn't mean you wear that middle America shit to work, son! This is FI-nance. FI as in "FIx me a drink, Jeeves." FI as in "FIlling my wallet with Ben-jamins." FI as in "FIckle with my private jets." Not FI as in "FIt really well when I tried it on at the mall in Piscataway." Ugh.

Whatever. Apparently, dude must have made sense of all our glares and cough-covered laughs or someone must have taken him aside and informed him there are no "casual" days around here, 'cause Josh shortly thereafter managed to find some passable, yet still vomit-inducing (Men's Wearhouse or some shit), clothes.

But then, a few days passed . . . and Josh didn't really do anything too stupid. I guess I was starting to come around. I started to think maybe I ought to give ol' Joshua a shot. I fig-ured, maybe consulting isn't all aligning boxes in PowerPoint and "value-adding" and ocean-boiling and ass-pounding. Maybe there was something more to it than lopsided pyramids and uninterpretable charts. But boy was I wrong . . . consulting really must be some serious horseshit.

Let me explain. Josh sits next to me, and I can see his screen. On around his sixth day, homeboy gets his first real assignment (some trivial EBITDA bridge analysis for a portfolio company), and he loads up the E (Excel), and tries to start getting to work. The stench of this kid's cluelessness was worse than the smell of the refrigerator in my Korean friend Matt's house—and kimchi smells horrendous. You could spot dude's lack of comfort from miles away, so it was actually physically painful to me at only three feet. I watched in horror as Josh busted out some dirty old hideously colored model to build off, and nearly passed out when I saw him start navigating.

Get this . . . HE WAS USING THE MOUSE!! . . . *WTF?!* I nearly shat myself with incredulity. I was so embarrassed that he was my colleague that I almost went and told one of the partners about the act of blasphemy I had just seen and that I would quit if some action wasn't taken. But I restrained myself. I had to calm down. I turned back to my computer, loaded up ESPN.com, took several deep breaths, and let myself get hypnotized by the ever-flashy Flash advertisements. After a moment, I knew what I had to do.

I turned and tapped Josh on the shoulder to get his attention. I didn't say a word, but my face said, "Yo . . . yeah you, McPoser." We locked eyes. I slowly and dramatically reached for my mouse cable. Staring him down, I methodically unplugged it from my computer's USB port. The cable came out slowly but smoothly and with its final, climactic release, I heard Josh gulp with fear.

I continued to glare at him as I started to "fly around." My eye-balls burned through his unweathered, sixty-hour-a-week-when-he-should-have-done-ninety face as I hid and unhid sheets and conditionally formatted and applied validation to cells with triple-nested conditional and indirect functions and then culminated by on-the-fly writing a macro that took my data and made it into a Marimekko (and we don't even use that shit!). I never turned to look at the screen, and my eyes never left his.

"Welcome to PE, bitch," I growled, crunching the last word as if making radio noises. Then, mildly irritated that I had re-vealed my lame TiVo-watching habits but proud of my mas-terful display, I turned back to my computer.

As I resumed my modeling, I could hear his hurried breaths, shaky and intermittent, and I knew that I had proven my point. Josh might have "exceeded expectations" at finger paint-ing and storytime over at True North, but his career in PE was:

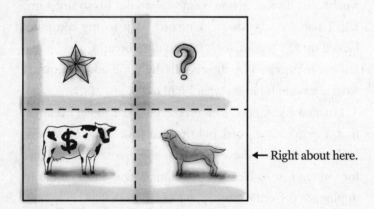

← Right about here.

PERFORMANCE REVIEW #3

1. Circle all the improper Banker fashion aspects of the following image:

2. Someone tells you that you are in a Banker city, but people are playing beer pong, even at the "nicest" bars. Where are you?

The correct answer: Chicago.

3. You have worked late but do not have a voucher for a car home. Do you:

    a. Take the subway.

    b. Take a cab.

    c. Sleep under your desk and take a car the next day.

The correct answer: c.

4. Which one of these is not like the others?

    a. *Liar's Poker*

    b. *Monkey Business*

    c. *Atlas Shrugged*

    d. *Freakonomics*

    e. *When Genius Failed*

The correct answer: d. It is crap pop-lit.

5. West Coast : East Coast :: Sell Side : _____

The correct answer: "Buy Side."

Entertainment

Best book ever:
The Unquestionable
Tightness of Banking.

Diversion

BANKING IS A rather consuming lifestyle. As such, Banker "free time" is limited and must be exploited fully when available. Bankers aren't like regular people who consume all forms of diversion; no, we are much more aware of what we like and don't waste our time "exploring" and messing around with other, trivial nonsense.

The track for Bankers generally goes: (Prep School/High School) → (Ivy League) → (Investment Banking) → (Private Equity / Hedge Funds) → (Greatness), and in between the legs of this process, we're blessed with several purely carefree months of joblessness. I have a nice hiatus coming before I start my new job in PE, and with several hundred K of my Bonus in the Bank, I'll travel across Europe, stopping only to pick up models and hang out on my buddy's yacht in Turkey. I'll wake up whenever I feel like it, hit the gym twice a day, and do whatever else seems like appropriate unemployed behavior until I start my new job and continue along my noble path.

Until then, I've basically got Sunday afternoons, when I grant myself a few hours to idle about. I usually sit on the couch with my laptop opened to Economist.com and browse the site casually, spotting relevant articles and critiquing their theses. At the same time, I bring up my DVR guide and look over the shows I have been too busy to watch.

TV Shows

TV is the most prole form of entertainment, but it allows me to "slum it" for a second, albeit in HD. In these moments, I feel like I'm tucked away in the asshole of America, eating microwave dinners and watching *Lost* with my ugly wife. Seconds into the reverie, I kill myself.

I review what I've got recorded and why I feel that I, as a Banker, connect with the shows:

Grey's Anatomy: Details the lives of those in medicine, an industry less thrilling than Banking, but it's entertaining for the fact that medical interns work just as hard as Analysts but get paid $30k a year and have to wear ugly blue jumpers.

The Sopranos: Mob boss Tony Soprano is obviously an instantly accessible character. His daily management issues and ruthless business tactics echo my own corporate lifestyle. This otherwise subtle connection is made overt in season six, episode four, when Paulie says, guido as ever: "Did you even know what your EBITDA is? Earnings Be-

fore Interest, Taxes, Depreciation, and Amortization—
gives the true picture of a company's profitability." Hell
yeah, it does, Paulie!

Entourage: I look at Vinny Chase and I see myself. We both
dominate our respective industries. He's slightly less sophisticated and pulls somewhat less attractive females, but
our charm and level of confidence are on the same level.
"Turtle!" I scream at my rotund Trader roommate, Jon,
and he obediently pokes his head out of his room.

Sex and the City: Confirms to Banker guys that we're the
only males women really desire, and confirms for the
Banker Chicks that they indeed have nothing in common
with normal females.

Gossip Girl: Affluent private school kids on the Upper East
Side of Manhattan do cocaine and party in hotels owned
by their parents. Also known as *Wall Street: The Early
Years.*

Web Sites

While I'm deciding what to watch, I browse through a few
other Web sites: Dealbreaker.com and Dealbook for some
relevant finance snark; WSJ.com to check in on my boy Ru-
pert Murdoch's daily musings; and the Drudge Report to
see how our "make a difference" think tank brethren in D.C.
are holding up. The comments on leveragedsellout.com are
particularly insightful today, but I end up on ESPN.com,
where I confirm that my Fantasy Football team is still the

greatest ever—Excel skills have many powerful applications.

Film

Nothing on my DVR engages me, so I consider popping in a movie. *Scarface*? Not really feeling the rags-to-riches story right now. Maybe *American Psycho*? A decent documentary. *Wall Street*? Perhaps, but I need something more relevant; the highly fictionalized themes of greed, corruption, and insider trading are no longer present in finance. Neither are Gordon Gekko–style suspenders.

I settle on *300*—superficially a story about the Battle of Thermopylae. I, however, understand it on a more allegorical level: We Bankers are Spartans waging daily war to protect our utopia from the invading savages. Whether it's a restructuring model for a multinational company or a massive pierced rhinoceros, I know we'll take it down.

I toss in the DVD and fast-forward to my favorite scene. Having just quizzed the Arcadians to unimpressive responses, King Leonidas looks back upon his company of men and screams: "WHAT IS YOUR PROFESSION?" And in my mind, the somewhat unintelligible gruff response is, in unison, "BANKER!"

I spear the air with my remote control.

But after only a few minutes, I grow bored of inactivity, and I get up and see that my roommate Jon is preparing to go golf. I leave the movie running and head into his room to check out the new clubs he bought for himself after a careless trading error turned out to be rather profitable for his group.

His room is messy. Blue shirts carpet the floor, and a Gatorade bottle full of dip spit sits on his desk next to an old baseball cap. His clubs are nice, though, especially his new Scotty Cameron. I pick it up and lazily putt a Morgan Stanley golf ball into an American Stock Exchange mug, and we joke about how the Amex is too shitty for anyone to ever drink from.

Along with squash, golf is one of the true Banker sports. Though it's now somewhat of a bourgeois game, I figure those accountants and high school gym teachers aren't really playing golf, they're just going through the motions and barely breaking eighty from the ladies' tees.

The Sales and Trading guys and the Buy Side hit the links a bit more than I do currently, but I relish any opportunity to breathe fresh air, smoke cigars, and flex wealth on sixteen-year-old cart girls. At Pine Valley or Bayonne, there's nothing like staring down some diabetic senior citizen and his kid who're trying to play through my Banker foursome. My eyes won't leave theirs as I'm balancing my phone on a conference call and simultaneously sinking a forty-foot putt. "Another birdie..." I'll announce casually. The old man and son will scurry off into the woods, embarrassed, and I hold up my phone to broadcast the applause of those on the call.

I ask my roommate about his night, and it turns out he

didn't go out; he stayed in and "read." Hmm. Knowing him, I figure that meant flipping through *Trader Monthly* in search of new Breitling ads or struggling through an abridged *Harry Potter*, but he has *American Pastoral* by Philip Roth on his bookshelf. "Literary, are we?" I ask before chucking the book across the room; not surprisingly, it lands on a blue shirt. I check out the rest of his bookshelf. It's got the real "literature"—the collective Banker Bible.

He has the appropriate Wall Street narratives:

Monkey Business: Two fratty associates relate their post-MBA time at DLJ, a prestigious Investment Bank now harvested by the less prestigious Credit Suisse. I chuckle thinking about one of them pissing under a table at a Christmas party. This is the only legit I-Banking memoir ever written.

Liar's Poker: A nonfiction member of the Banker canon that relates the author's years as a bond salesman in the 1980s. Although he went to Princeton, Michael Lewis is not really that Banker, having studied art history and currently living in New Orleans "writing." Regardless, the book is epic because Lewis is aware of his personal shortcomings and focuses his efforts on the real "Big Swinging Dicks"—Lewis Ranieri, John Gutfreund, Michael Milken, et al.

When Genius Failed: The Rise and Fall of Long-Term Capital Management: I recall bringing up this book as a favorite in several interviews. A detailed description of the clusterfuck that ensued when quant-based Long-Term Capital Management screwed up the entire economy and had to be saved by the rest of The Street, it reminds us to curse stupid math PhDs and computer science guys and anyone who trusts them with money. Originally titled *Quants Suck: Get Back in the Back Office.*

There's no Dewey Decimal System, but Jon's reference section is grouped thematically and also well stocked. I see the basic shit every Econ major alludes to: *A Random Walk Down Wall Street* and *Options, Futures, and Other Derivatives* (the Hull book). And next to some CliffsNotes for *Ulysses,* he has several Vault Guides—they look fitting next to each other, both easy ways out for those who don't care about really understanding anything.

My hand runs across *The Art of War* and finally *Atlas Shrugged,* a Banking manifesto cloaked in an ostensibly philosophical novel. A tribute to society's reliance on diligence and rational self-interest, the symbolism of finance isn't even veiled. It's obvious that we are Titan, and society would collapse, leaving the "looters" and "moochers" doomed if Bankers shrugged.

There's also a set of Trading books I haven't read: *Reminiscences of a Stock Operator, Market Wizards,* and a few others.

How funny is it that there's a library in the locker room, I think, and laugh.

But I'm curious: "Which one of these has helped you the most?" I ask Jon.

Spitting into the Gatorade bottle he's still drinking from, he points at *The Theory of Poker* by David Sklansky.

It seems like a joke at first, but it's not. When I sit at a table, I prefer it to be at a nightclub with a set of models as opposed to a bunch of fat dudes in Atlantic City, but the importance of poker on Wall Street is undeniable. Gambling is fairly core to our personalities. We have money, some of which must go into higher-risk investments such as gaming—it's basic portfolio theory. Like any rational human beings, we hunt positive EV (expected value) situations and capitalize on them.

Finance has produced some of the best poker players ever. Erik Seidel, Alan Goehring, Bill Chen, and others have all worked in or around Wall Street. We're used to taking positions worth millions of dollars on a daily basis, so sitting down at a $1,000/$2,000 No-Limit cash game is really kind of a joke—even in the Big Game, the stakes are always negligible. In a contest largely dictated by one's ability to play smart and not get off balance due to swings, Bankers are un-tiltable.

I leave Jon's room and head into the shower, where Kiehl's takes on a residual nightclub smell, heads up. On the way, the sounds of the movie get my attention, and as I walk by the TV, I see some Bankers pushing a huge elephant off the side of a cliff. *Poor earnings this quarter?* I figure. I remember that my roommate's firm and others (such as Susquehanna and Lehman Brothers) actually require their employees to play poker; they give them a set amount of money and monitor their performance. There's even a Wall Street World Series of Poker, which I imagine makes the original look like a bunch of construction workers playing low-stakes Go Fish in an unfinished basement in Schenectady.

Enjoying the comfort of my own bathroom, I remember a prop bet I made with a colleague when I first got into Banking. He had already been in the office for twenty-four hours, and I bet him $500 that he couldn't last a week without leaving. It wasn't about the money; it was about perseverance. He showered in the gym, slept under a conference table, and had new clothes delivered to him daily by an obedient Brooks Brothers shop girl. Turns out a week was no big deal; he had gone nine days just the month before without even realizing it.

$$\$\ \$\ \$$

After I've showered and selected a casual weekend outfit of jeans and a polo, I'm eager to get back to being productive. The upcoming summer will be relaxing and these few free hours were fun, but I just don't feel right unless I'm out there working, breathing life into the economy.

Jon's leaving for his golf outing just as I'm taking off, and we make our exit together. I must have neglected to shut off the TV, because *300* is still playing in the background when we depart. As the door closes, I hear: "Bankers! Prepare for glory!"

INSIDER INFO WITH CHRIS, A MARKET MAKER

I did exactly two things in college—trade via a personal satellite dish I didn't really need just so I could be like Ken Griffin, founder of Citadel Group, and play No-Limit Texas Hold 'Em. I'm not the luckiest person, but based on pure skill and Trading sense, I am able to win with all sorts of hands.

Last month, I was at the Bellagio in Vegas, and I sat down at a table with a bunch of pros, including Phil Hellmuth. I didn't give a shit who they were. From the get-go I was playing super-loose and aggressive, like we Traders are known to. I threw my cash in everyone's face. Some of the players called me a "donkey," and an old lady watching made weird fishy noises as she writhed about the casino floor. Whatever, I was *in their heads.*

On one hand, I was dealt 10-2 offsuit in position, and Phil Hellmuth had raised big pre-flop. My hand was quite horrible for the average player, but I paused for a moment and stared at The Brat, using the intuition I learned Trading to pierce his soul. I raised him all in.

As it turns out, I rivered a royal flush on the last card, and Phil's suited ace-king didn't hold up. I could tell from Phil's reaction that in all his games of poker, he had never faced such a formidable opponent.

continued

"Who the fuck *are* you?" he said, out of breath and barely whispering.

I cocked my head to the side slightly and pulled down my sunglasses so he could soak me in.

"I'm the Michael Milken of poker," I responded matter-of-factly.

He contorted his face, now even more confused.

I sighed at his ignorance of the 1980s high-yield bond market and explained: *"I win with junk."*

FACT #14

This is how we do it on Broad & Wall, bitch!

Partying

MOST PEOPLE LACK a fundamental understanding of partying. What generally happens is that an individual and his friends will find a party niche in which they become comfortable and then try to exploit that niche for as much fun as possible. This thinking is severely flawed.

Bankers, on the other hand, focus on optimizing across a set of discrete party factors, leading to the greatest overall output in both the long term and a given session. It's basic linear programming, a mathematical technique frequently applied to economics. The practice involves optimizing an "objective function" based on a set of "constraints." As Bankers, we're trying to maximize drinks, quality music, dancing, and, of course, girls. Our only real constraint is time.

We solve for this function by distributing our time appropriately across a set of very defined venues.

$$\$\$\$$$

In e-mail, Bankers are masters of the fragment: "Will get back to you ASAP." "Feedback strong." "Now." To achieve even greater efficiency, these phrases are often just inserted as the subject of e-mails with no bodies.

On Fridays, I receive around thirty e-mails from friends discussing the night's activities. We still use fragments, but the subject lines are slightly different: "Roof coming off tonight." "Game faces on." And, my personal favorite, "Better bring the umbrella."

These e-mails get me amped to roll hard, and with my game face on, I'll be sitting on the edge of my Aeron chair, fueled and eager to explode out onto the night. My foot taps restlessly on my ergonomic foot pillow as I procrastinate efficiently, and when it's around 10:30 and the work has abated, I'll know it's go-time.

We have a new Analyst in our group, Chris, who's been slaving away dutifully, and I figure he's due for a proper Banker night out. I walk over to his chair and find him passed out with a hand on his mouse and an almost-clever Microsoft Excel screensaver bouncing around his monitor. *Good thought, poor implementation,* I think. He's peaceful, in a pathetic, hobo-asleep-on-the-street kind of way. I touch his shoulder, and he leaps to life. "I'll have those numbers in a few hours!" he shouts, shuffling around nonexistent papers.

I calm him down and let him know that I am not actually our VP, but his instincts are developing well. After five to ten minutes of explanation, he's finally convinced. "Time to roll!" I notify, loosening my tie slightly. But he resists, blaming a mountain of work.

I won't stand for it.

"Chris," I advise him gently. "It's not all about work." I am a sage imparting knowledge to a naive pupil.

He stares at me confused, as if I've just uttered the unimaginable.

"It's about *us*," I explain, using my index finger to point between him and me—two young financiers in the greatest city in the universe. I pause, reflecting on how manly I made that otherwise questionable statement sound. I continue, with gravity: "It's about *this*." And I point a finger in the air and circle, motioning to our entire building.

I want him to comprehend the true meaning of working on Wall Street. He needs to grasp the work hard–roll hard duality that makes our lives so distinct and amazing. I bring my arms together, ball up my fists, and clench them close to my chest. "It's about Banking," I finish. And I catch a glimmer of understanding in his eyes.

Bars

We start the night at a bar near the office. Their happy hours start late, and as we walk into the packed space, it's obvious that a drink special held at five o'clock, or six, or whenever regular people get out of work would have fallen flat on its face. *Know your customer,* I think, pondering whether they also have a happy hour at 3:30 a.m. on Tuesday nights—another popular time Bankers leave work in need of a drink.

One might think that Bankers wouldn't deign to go to bars, where the world's poor, depressed, and ugly gather to discuss relationship issues, bitch about gasoline prices, and toast "to friendship." But for us, bars aren't welcoming meeting grounds or places where people know our names; they're places of utility. Bars facilitate maximum drinking and, if selected properly, will offer a good mix of Banker music and dancing.

Established Banker bars are great, but every Banker also frequents a few truly gritty dives where we can get a brief lens into the dismal life of an average man. It's an experience, like being taken on a field trip to an inner-city school. I'm more open-minded now than when I was eight, but I still can't help pointing and whispering about how deprived and sad everyone looks.

I organize our night via numerous texts and e-mails on my BlackBerry as Chris rambles on about how he's enjoying the firm's culture. "Face time's over, kid." I tell him. We have a few options: a friend who lives nearby is having a rooftop party we could swing through; there's also a benefit for some noble cause going on, where we could don tuxedos and help better society.

Benefits

Banks as institutions and Bankers individually are huge sponsors of benefits, and as a result, the affairs are often schmooze sessions for Wall Street's finest. They include but are not limited to: dinners, live music, open bars, dancing, and auctions (both silent and open-outcry). When Bankers get into a bidding war over a certain piece, the fervor takes on the intensity of a Trading pit, each participant bumping up the price with unrelenting conviction—that's how much we care about making a difference.

I'm not really feeling either option, but the word *rooftop* piques Chris's interest. I ignore him and decide that since it's Chris's first real night out, I'll call up a few friends and tell them to meet us at one of the Meatpacking District's hottest nightclubs, in true Banker fashion.

Clubs

As the lights of the heaters hovering above the red carpet become visible, I hear Chris let out a worried sigh. He's spotted the line—a mass of people winding around the block composed of those lacking enough merit to get into the club without first standing outside for forty-five minutes.

I pay it no mind. I spot my friends and walk over to them. Chris isn't behind me anymore, and I see that he's started to make his way to the back of the queue. We fall all over one another in laughter, slapping and socking arms.

"Chris. Get over here!" I scream across the street.

"First day on the job?" someone asks.

He jogs back and stands with us, doe-eyed, as we briefly chat up the bouncer. I instruct him to focus, as if this were his first day of training and I were a partner giving a speech that would prep him for the rest of his life. "Pay attention, Chris," I coach, motioning for him to watch closely. We buy bottles.

Bottle Service

Bottle service, table service, or the act of "getting bottles" consists of purchasing one or more bottles of top-shelf liquor at a rather inflated price and getting seated at one's own table. This product was designed to play to the Banker's soft spots. It essentially removes the need to wait in line, saving time; prime, elevated status within the club is instantly achieved; and it's an easy way to drop several thousand dollars and broadcast the fact that you are doing so.

The convenience of bottles is so great that I've adapted it to the rest of my life, whenever I'm hoping to skirt a queue and get prompter service. Long line at the post office? I'll take a bottle, Mr. Postman. Starbucks too crowded in the morning? Two bottles—Americanos. This practice might not initially be universally understood, but shoving a few hundred dollars in someone's face tends to get the desired effect. And it just feels good.

We roll into the club, five dudes deep, and I wink and silently hand-gun some Long Island meathead and his overly made-up girlfriend. "That B– in Econ 101 at junior college really stings now, doesn't it?" my glare conveys, and the girlfriend looks at us longingly. Meathead's huge muscles sag, rendered irrelevant.

The glasses at our table are set up in an elaborate configuration around an ice bucket and two carafes of juice, orange and cranberry. This situation has overwhelmed his senses, and Chris physically can't speak, he's in such a state of shock. As the waitress pours our first round, I hear the subtle clink of our private section being closed off with velvet rope, and the not-so-subtle clink of us toasting (not to "friendship").

I don't know how many times I've gotten bottle service; it's not worth counting. Once I even went with my Korean colleague Chang to this nightclub in K-town called Camel. The bottles were Johnny Black then, not Grey Goose, and they came out with an ornate plate of fruit: watermelon, honeydew, and cantaloupe. At Camel, Chang was no longer timid and docile; he was confident, talked up girls easily, and had several clawing all over him, hanging on his every word. I felt like I was watching a movie of my life, and Chang was the anime character playing me.

Back in the real world, I'm the one flanked by gorgeous females. Even after all these times of bottle service, the sensation of our lofty status in the club is exhilarating. I spot a VP of mine, The Game, at a table with suboptimal position, and he raises his glass to me, enviously. Then I look next to me and see Chris, who is now gawking at a lanky, blond girl in a tube top she's pawning off as a dress. She's a reasonable target, albeit standard. "Get to it," I tell him, but he brushes it off, assuring me that he's "all good." His edification in my hands, I lift him up by the arm, take him over to the blonde, and say, shouting slightly over the music: "Hi. This is Chris." I point at Chris. Then I deliver the silver bullet, slowly and articulately: "He works in fin*n*ance."

I let the magic phrase sink in, and within seconds, her face is covered in a bright red blush. The true power of Banker Game shows itself yet again.

Banker Game

Banker Game is unstoppable. Genuine self-confidence is a quality that pickup artists across the world try to capture and teach; it is also a quality all Bankers innately possess. We exude a certain magnetism that women just can't resist, and they flock to us like idiotic investors to Jim Cramer's stock recommendations.

Most normal guys have to focus on "openers" or "lines" to get women to talk to and be interested in them. But Chris didn't even have to form a complete sentence after meeting his girl. I looked over a few minutes later and could read her lips saying, as if she were in some Wall Street version of *Jerry Maguire:* "You had me at fin*n*ance."

The night goes well for all of us, and we're soon swatting away girls like they're headhunters.

I briefly think about the bottle service e-mail that's going to be sent tomorrow. It will be another fragment—"Came to $2,500"—from whoever ends up taking down the bill tonight, and we'll know where to send our share of the tab. When we used to go out with my Consultant roommate, Rob, we would make bets on how long it would take him to respond to the bottle service e-mail, haggling about the price. He was worse than Banker Chicks, who at least don't even offer to pay when we go out after a work event. Rob, on the other hand, would send out a response like: "Actually, guys, I only really drank 2.35 drinks last night while you all had 4 each, so I really should not have to cough up as much as everyone else . . ." And then I would win the bet, because I knew it would never take a Consultant more than five seconds to start bitching about money.

I'm speaking to the girl on my left, and it's instinctive, as "modeling" always is for me. I'm not in Excel, but I multitask, now considering whether I should let Chris go home with the blonde or whether we should leave to experience yet another crucial aspect of the Banker Partying Paradigm.

He still hasn't been to a strip club, and I want to gauge his reaction to a $50 ATM fee and the marriage proposal of an Eastern European illegal alien. But I reason that he may enjoy the experience more when it's a group-wide thing, and he can expense himself a private room. Chris also hasn't yet been a part of Banker Karaoke, and I know he needs to be trained to give a strong presentation, even if he has no idea what the words are.

I look over and see that he's finally at ease and chatting away with his girl, and I realize we will have more nights to party together; he's not a bad kid. Plus, I'd feel like a cock block going in there at this point. I rework that phrase: I'd feel like a white knight, going in to buy a strategic shareholding of a company to "save" it from takeover. I don't want to be either at this point because, as The Game loves to say, "After a hard day of M&A, there's nothing like bringing home some T&A."

Chris motions to get my attention. One arm around the blonde, he points between us, around us, and finally pulls his fist close to his chest. *"Us." "This."* "Banking," he says, in turn. And I see more than a glimmer of understanding in his eyes.

INSIDER INFO WITH SHANE, A BOUNCER

Bankers are the best customers, hands down.

One time, a Banker tipped me $1,000 just for remembering his name.

I'll see a group of like eight of them come in and sometimes only six will leave (each with his own harem of girls, of course). Do the other two helicopter off the roof or use some special Banker magic?

I've even got the lingo down now. They'll show up, and I'll say: "How's the deal flow, boys?" Then it's: Wink. Nod. $200 in my pocket.

And get this, last week this guy came through and started dancing on the bar like he was in *Coyote Ugly*. Kinda gay, right? Afterward, he came outside and started doing a "back of the envelope valuation" and started saying some shit about putting in a "generous bid" on the bar. I don't know what the hell any of that means, and I didn't see any envelope, but I guess you can do whatever you want when you roll that deep.

What planet are these dudes from, anyway? More important, do they need bouncers on that planet? I bet they tip pretty well there.

CASE STUDY: THE BENEFIT

This is a tribute to philanthropy.

After learning all the compelling aspects of the industry, you might wonder, "What's really the *best* part about being in finance?"

"Is it the jet-setting lifestyle?"

—That's a small part.

"Is it the opportunity to work on complex problems in a stimulating environment surrounded by peers who push your boundaries intellectually?"

—Somewhat.

And, the inevitable dose of naiveté, of course: "Is it the money?"

—Hardly. How shameful for you to even bring that up.

So then, what is the best part about working in finance? If Bankers aren't overly concerned with the bling, the glam, or the science, what is it? What, in the end, is the aspect that makes it all so worthwhile?

That aspect is, indisputably, *the kids.*

That's right—*the kids.* Bankers donate to charities and foundations across the board, from curing multiple sclerosis to saving the environment to developing the $100 laptop, but more so than any other cause, they make sure to help out *the kids.*

And because of the way Bankers tend to organize their

charitable donations, what merits the cost is, quite appropriately: the benefit.

Let me explain.

I once went with my MD to a benefit where he was on the board of a youth foundation and watched him buy a hideous $50,000 painting in a live auction. The painting was done by a graduate of the youth center and can be summed up as Banksy meets thirteen years of heroin addiction meets fourth-grade special-ed watercoloring. But my MD didn't even bat an eye when the bidding started. He bought that painting for $50k, took it home, and it stayed in his garage until his eighteen-year-old son put it up on the wall of his dorm next to his "Beer: Rounding Out the Hourglass Since 1886" poster. And why did he buy it? Because it was the right thing to do.

Another time, some of us were at a benefit for leukemia, and the little cancerous kids came around asking for people to sponsor them by buying $100 gold ribbons. When this happened, did we make our fingers into cross signs and shun the genetically unsound, shielding ourselves from their malignant afflictions? No, we all bought gold ribbons, and we wore them proudly on our lapels. Yes, we were a little nervous the pins might damage our fabric, but it still felt good to help the cause.

Bankers even go the extra mile for *the kids*. I've recently become a member of the board of a nonprofit started by me and my peers that helps youths in Africa somehow or the other. Every three months, I dedicate two hours to organizing a benefit that brings together young professionals from all over the city for a night of fun, dancing, and, most important, lifesaving. Sure, being on said board might help with B-school applications and, sure, girls generally tend to come wearing dresses that look more like onesies (hot!), but that's just fringe. It's not the sloppy titties and the remarkably easy hookups that fill me with joy, it's that overwhelming communal feeling of "We're doing everything within our power to make a difference." And that's unbeatable.

You see, in life you can try to better things by joining the Peace Corps or volunteering at a hospital or making some other sort of Bowdoin College–style individualized gesture, or you can get into finance and be part of a *movement*. I recently read that for every $10k collected at a proper benefit, $1 ends up going to charity. That's not bad at all considering the high cost of decent caterers, cover bands, Grey Goose, and Sotheby's auctioneers. That one dollar is like cereal and powdered milk for a month for a small village. Hey kiva.org, kinda lookin' like shit now, huh?

But the best for me is that sometimes, when I'm in a car home, I'll have this recurring work-induced hallucination/reverie. In my vision, I see a little orphaned tribal boy in a desolate community. But my boy's got spirit in him, and he's clawing to save his last bit of protease inhibitors before they're ripped away by a gangster with an AK-47. Then, empty-handed, the little boy turns and stares at me with big, pleading eyes.

I reach out in my dream and touch the boy on the shoulder

with a firm, paternal grip. His eyes are no longer pleading; they're now hopeful, waiting for me to rescue him from his condition. At that point, I say to him, encouragingly: "Don't worry, Dikembe, breakfast's on Blackstone."

And that's the best part about working in finance.

FACT #15

Every little deal
I do is magic.

Music

WITHOUT QUESTION, BANKER music is the best music. The sound we appreciate is the kind that touches your soul, moves your feet, and either evokes profound thought or provides a cool dulling sensation—whichever is appropriate at the time. It is the music that is able to capture a movement, mentality, and culture and preserve them indefinitely, wrapped up in 4/4 time. Like the Bankers Whol listen to it, it's raw.

Banker music is the exact opposite of everything pretentious, faux, and "artistic" in the music industry. It is not "abstract," it is not "edgy," it is not "hubristic," and it is certainly not "independent." Banker music is like the companies we deal with: dedicated to generating profits.

Our iPods are filled with tracks that reflect our common goals and sensibilities. Bankers do not do "everything in moderation." We do "everything in excess." And we pump songs throughout the day that echo our core values.

Underground Hip-Hop

I have a "Banking" playlist that I listen to throughout the day. I had to play with it for a few months before finally getting it perfect, but one day, all the pieces and genres fell together in what was a true "soundtrack for my life."

I woke up to Notorious B.I.G.'s "Juicy." "Fuck all you hos," he started casually, and a steady snare set the cadence as I threw off the covers. Unlike Biggie, who sold drugs in the ghetto before finding rap, I always knew I was going to be a Banker. But we're not that different, he and I, and as his deep grumble continued, it became my intro instead of his:

"This life is dedicated to all the professors who gave me my thesis award. To all the people who interviewed me and wined and dined me until I accepted my offer when I was just trying to make sure I got the best comp so I could feed my prestige. And all the Bankaz without struggle. You know what I'm sayin'?"

"It's all good, baby baby." We paused before the beat dropped, and I mouthed the lyrics to the verse along with him.

"It was all a dream . . . I used to watch *Squawk Box* as a teen / Goldman Sachs and Blackstone up in the limousine . . ."

"Schwarzman's picture on my wall!" I said out loud. Big Poppa and I shared a moment, celebrating ambition.

$$$

It was a regular Monday, and the hip-hop built my excitement as I got ready for the work week. The symbolism was subtle and unpronounced but powerful.

In the bathroom, "Money, Cash, Hoes" blared as I scraped the multiple, pulsating blades of a Mach 3 Fusion over my face. The melodic whistle of "Big Pimpin'" accompanied my buttoning up a pink, checkered custom-tailored shirt and tucking it into my black pants. Pulling on my loafers, I hummed along with the stereo, subconsciously modifying the song's chorus to be: "Mo money, fewer problems."

I slung a messenger bag over my shoulder, grabbed my iPod out of its dock, and stuffed my ears with its earbuds. As I picked up my *Wall Street Journal* on the way out of my building, I saw an ink sketch of 50 Cent in a baseball cap above an article about Glacéau's board of directors. *Waddup, 50!* I thought, and suddenly the connection between hip-hop and finance was not so cryptic.

Bankers really are "true heads" that appreciate underground hip-hop from the likes of Biggie, Jay-Z, Nelly, and Ludacris. Rappers have "whips," and Bankers have "black cars." Rhyme slayers wear Sean John and deal slayers wear Turnbull & Asser. Which came first: Westside connection or Buyside connection? Who knows. In the end, we're all just straight thugs who end up having to get dirty for "the paper."

The rap had made me feel particularly "street," and so I rode the subway. As I read my skillfully folded-up newspaper to the sound of "It's All About the Benjamins," a mass of people encroached on my personal space. It wasn't a comfortable "look over my shoulder to inspect analysis" infringement but a painful "I have to look at your $15 jacket up close" offense. I finally emerged, free.

My steps in sync with the bass drum, I walked along the Financial District's streets to a slow, powerful beat and high-pitched violin. I reached my building and got swept into a line of people breezing through the spiral doors. Making it through, I was welcomed by the taste of crisp, oxygenated air and the chorus of none other than "Gangsta's Paradise."

Well played, Coolio, I thought, slapping my ID down on the sensor in time with a high hat.

For the rest of the morning and early afternoon, I transitioned to pop. The music market is fairly efficient, and unlike the stock market, hunting for undervalued bands has only marginal returns. There are no hidden John Mayers or U2s. No Dave Matthews is buried below undervalued physical assets. As such, pop music is the only case where Bankers trust the majority.

Pop Music

After an hour or so, I got up to take a chart over to Word Processing. I left my iPod behind, and I only had my mental stereo system as I walked by the various people in the office.

Meredith, a Banker Chick, was wearing pink headphones and trying not to chair-dance as she simultaneously browsed fashion sites and jammed on a spreadsheet. I passed, and she deftly alt-tabbed away *Women's Wear Daily* in favor of a 10-K, but her head still bobbed back and forth happily as she lip-synced Madonna: *"Material, material!"* In my mind, I first heard "Baby Got Back," but it was quickly replaced by Queen's more appropriate "Fat Bottomed Girls."

My Associate had a look of strain and discomfort on his face as he talked into his headset. In his free ear, an earbud was connected to his iPod, and I imagined that he was being soothed by the likes of Kelly Clarkson, Michelle Branch, or Natasha Bedingfield—he's that kind of guy. All three of these women have created epic Banker tracks, but not without the aid of a techno remix.

I rode the elevator with Ted, a less-than-bright Analyst with some identity issues. He had started reading Pitchfork Media a month or so ago and now fancied himself to be on the bleeding edge of indie rock music. "You heard the new Bloc Party album?" he asked me, proud and eager to showcase his hipness.

I didn't even acknowledge his existence. This was another one of his "finds" Ted would office DJ until someone came by and pulled his wrinkle-free Brooks Brothers shirt over his head as if they were in an office hockey game. Real Bankers don't follow his Third-Tier music, because, like Ted, it definitely doesn't belong here.

I finally made it to Word Processing, and Tania had on huge, Bose noise-canceling-style jug headphones. She was entranced, her spirit suffocated by minutiae. You have to be at some advanced stage of insanity to manage that job, and I wondered what tortured brand of music she was listening to. Deathrock? Emo? A capella?

After passing off the chart, I got back to my desk and, as a sardonic tribute to her, Justin Timberlake's "Cry Me a River" came on.

Eighties Music

The day progressed without event, and in the afternoon, I did some modeling in Excel while listening to the most consummate Banker music in existence: eighties. I wish I had been a year or two older back in the eighties, just when young professionals were gaining buying power and affluence; I could have shown those guys a thing or two about rolling hard. But now, Bankers are even better off, and eighties music still facilitates our celebration of indulgence.

Running my thumb across the iPod's wheel, I became aware that the very names of eighties bands screamed of number crunching: the Cure, the Fixx, a-ha, Extreme, and, somehow, even Rick Springfield. I worked at a blinding pace and dipped back briefly ten more years in musical history to feel like a digital version of Billy Joel's "Piano Man." Another Analyst walked by and spotted me using a shortcut key he didn't know. *"Show me show me show me how you do that trick,"* his awestruck eyes sang. Was there an eighties song titled "Fuck you, no!" I wondered?

I was using the Capital Asset Pricing Model to value

companies, and I similarly defined the Banker Song Assessment Model for music.

$$BSAM = M + C_{CR}(L + \tfrac{1}{D})$$

The model has four variables:

1. *Melody (M):* To be a true Banker song, a minimum of thirty people at a party must be able to sing along to the tune at the same time, and a minimum of fifty others must be able to mouth the lyrics while the song plays.

   Scoring: The melody variable is assigned a number from 0 to 5 based on how many days after one hears the song that it is still stuck in one's head. A score of 5 takes about a month. If the melody is forgotten the same day, the entire BSAM score drops to 0 and there is no way the song could be a hit.

2. *Lyrics (L):* As heady, erudite listeners, the lyrics in Banker music are crucial, and this variable is weighted heavily as a result.

   Scoring: For a given song, *L* is calculated by counting the number of occurrences of words from the following set: *bling, baby, love, prayer, ice* (not followed by water), *bitch* (all conjugations), *South, umbrella,* and *magic*.

3. *Rhythm (C$_{CR}$):* Bankers need to be able to get "crunk" to their music. C$_{CR}$, the coefficient of crunkness, is assigned based on how crazy one can get to a given song. C$_{CR}$ is not dependent on the beats per minute of a song or how "urban" the rhythm is; those are irrelevant.

Scoring: Like *M,* the coefficient of crunkness must be observed. For the test, a set of Bankers is studied. Each is given ten shots of SoCo and lime and an unopened can of beer to hold in his hands while he listens to the song in a padded room. After the song has played, the can is opened, and the trajectory of the explosion is measured. The distances are averaged across all test subjects for a given song, and the results of the test are stored in a reference table.

4. *Duration (D):* Bankers don't have time to sit around waiting five minutes for a chorus. "Bohemian Rhapsody" is the only exception and is given a fractional score to inflate its score even further.

I ate dinner listening to "If I Ruled the World" by Nas, my mind conveniently removing the conditional tense from the lyrics. Afterward, I cranked on a pitch book with a couple other Analysts and an Associate. Most of the VPs and MDs had cleared out of the office, leaving us together in the bullpen. *We're alone now,* and music of all different genres blared out of someone's speakers, encouraging us along.

"Save Tonight" was followed by Green Day's "Basket Case." Ted's eyes rolled back in his head as he formatted a pie chart, affectionately whispering the words to "I Wanna Be Sedated." Matchbox Twenty told us the time at "3 a.m.," and we finally e-mailed a file off to our MD.

It seemed unlikely he'd respond before morning, and a heady wave of conquest crashed over the group. Some clever person cued up "We Are the Champions." Fists were in the air and Meredith was head-banging and playing air guitar on a table when our MD called back five minutes later, disappointed: some numbers didn't "foot."

Fucking Footloose *soundtrack,* I thought.

Hearing my MD's angry voice, I couldn't help but imagine him lying in bed with his Deal Trophy wife, "Stacy's Mom," but there was no time to consider her; we were screwed.

"Shattered Dreams" actually did not play and neither did "Hot in Herre," because there was nothing in the air except everyone else's worry. I wasn't overly concerned, and we all pored over the figures, trying to pinpoint the problem. My Associate flipped out and walked into the hallway, singing to himself therapeutically.

After forty-five minutes, I spotted the error nestled deep inside a formula on the fifteenth tab of a huge model. Sick. I didn't make a huge deal of it but sent off a quick note to my Associate, CCing our MD. " 'Since U Been Gone,' " I started the e-mail, blowing up my Associate's spot. "I found the issue."

I had queued up "You're the Best" from *The Karate Kid* right after I noticed the bug, and as I victoriously clicked "Send," it reached the hook. I nearly crane-kicked the monitor.

$$ \$ \ \$ \ \$ $$

It was now 4:30 a.m., and the workday was over. I headed out into our version of dusk and grabbed a car.

"Take Me Home Tonight!" Eddie Money belted through

the earphones I jammed into the driver's ear. His English struggled, but he understood.

The twenty-hour playlist ran its course as I peeled off my loafers and collapsed onto the bed. Right before I shut it off, it looped, and "Juicy" came back on.

I listened to the first few words again and looked back for a second on a rather regular day in Banking. It was all a dream, and now I'm livin' it.

INSIDER INFO WITH EMINEH

I'm part Banker, part freestyle battle rapper
Wrote this on my BlackBerry while I was sleeping on the
   crapper
You know I never leave the house unless I'm looking
   rather dapper.
'Cause I'm the illest MC from Greenwich, CT
A six-figga jigga, and I'm only twenty-three.
Spend all my money on slick clothes and blow
Go ahead, I dare you to try to discount these lyrical flows.

Sent from my BlackBerry Wireless Device . . .

This e-mail communication is privileged, confidential, or otherwise protected by disclosure and is intended only for the individuals or entities named above and any others who have been specifically authorized to receive it . . .

FACT #16

Back that cash up.
Dance

ALONG WITH MUSIC, dance is another way Bankers demonstrate that, in addition to having society's strongest left brains, our right brains trump everyone else's whenever we deign to use them.

At a certain level, Banker dancing is similar to traditional dancing: it's entertaining, primarily performed when intoxicated, and serves to attract the opposite sex. But like everything we do, our dancing is sculpted to maximize utility, so our moves are much more robust and efficient than any normal two-step.

On occasion, I'll put aside the club scene and take a night where I can really get crunk. These nights, my roommates and I will go to a nearby bar to put on what we refer to as "a clinic."

We begin by pre-gaming at our place. The night has no intention of being elegant or extravagant. It's the kind of night where we play quarters and other binge-drinking games at our apartment, get smashed, and head out. I throw on my

Princeton ring, because it shines in the light when I'm holding a drink in my hand and dancing, and as soon as Jon has
done a CCC Walk—a Crip walk tribute to poorly rated
bonds—across the kitchen floor, we roll.

In the cab, we review the rules:

1. Every bittie loves a Banker. It doesn't matter whether a
girl is with her mom, brother, or boyfriend, she will leave
anyone to be with us.

2. No broke girls, no Banker Chicks—mutually inclusive
and self-exploratory.

3. Bankers do not do ethnic dances. The salsa, merengue,
bhangra, tango, and so on are never, ever implemented by
Bankers. This is not out of ignorance or racism, but rather
because these dances are trivial and ordinary when compared to our own.

There are several bars in Manhattan that are perfect places to
roll hard, and we arrive at one of them, buzzed and ready to
tear the roof off.

I enter casually, surveying the scene and soaking in the
ambiance. The bar is situated immediately to the right, and a
thin walkway leads to the open back area. There's a good girl-
guy ratio, and the crowd is mostly young professional with
some B&T sprinkled in. I spot a guy in an AGP-ass Armani
Exchange shirt. *So B-list,* I think, but the bar is acceptable for
tonight's purposes.

From behind me, Jon's deep voice booms over the music, announcing our arrival. "Wall Street in da house!" he booms. And I lean back slightly and do a mini roof-raise.

The music is Banker. We make our way toward the bar to the sounds of "Eye of the Tiger," and although a thick crowd of people is trying to get drinks, I throw up one finger in the air victoriously.

This is my favorite dance move, as it informs everyone that not only am I Top Tier and top 1 percent of society, but also that I was valedictorian of my high school. For added effect, I'll often put my extended index finger in some guy's face or throw up both hands in emphasis. An envious viewer might see this prestigious move and raise a meek finger to mimic it, but his action will go unnoticed, like a Back Office guy trying to hail a black car.

My message has been sent loud and clear, and I've established my presence. Guys and girls alike look at me enviously. *An easy crowd,* I think. Gopal, overeager as ever, says: "Hostile takeover?" I slap him swiftly across the face.

Three Stellas in hand, we head to the back area where a group of girls is dancing. Normal guys do "laps" around the bar and contemplate their approaches, but we aren't normal guys.

On cue, the DJ tosses on the International Banking Anthem: "Josie's on a vacation far away!" belts out of the speakers.

Everyone goes wild, throwing up their arms and oohing and aahing as if they had written the song themselves.

Within moments, I have a bidder who meets my asking price—a cute brunette in a red sundress, a reasonable partner. We dance, and she seems mystified by my moves. She tries her best to keep up, but I sense inexperience and forcefully pull her in for a brief version of a move I usually do with work, Eighteen-Hour Grind.

I spin her around multiple times so she feels like a ballerina and reel her in for the inverted version, crossing her arms across her stomach. We rock back and forth for half an hour or so.

The virtuoso DJ continues to please, inciting similarly profound reactions with every new track. He skillfully mixes David Bowie into Puff Daddy into Elton John back into Bon Jovi, topping things off with some Enrique. I look over to inspect who this wildly talented artist is, and I find he's wearing a tight black T-shirt and a leather vest. He has several piercings and tattoos to match his thick gold necklace, but he's so *in touch* with our culture that I can't help but tilt my head and think: *Banker?*

As the chorus to "Hungry Like the Wolf" comes on, I can feel my partner's thin stomach grumble slightly through her dress. I turn to face her. "Resist the temptation!" my eyes encourage. She nods sheepishly in resolution.

Tim McGraw's "Something Like That" gets played, and I instinctively look across the dance floor at Jon—Trading is so country. He's doing the only move his less-than-lithe body can manage, but, like a good Trader, he's not afraid to Buy the Dips, and takes his twist down real low. His blue button-down has a stain on it, but it doesn't affect his game. He's pilfered someone else's girl, and we virtual high-five each other across the dance floor in celebration of rule #1.

The brunette has been entertaining, but when the Jackson 5 comes on, it's time to go solo.

"ABC. Easy as 1 2 3," they sing playfully, as a circle forms around me.

I have the entire bar's attention. My body is stiff, and my rigid movements make it appear as if I'm doing the Robot. But the keen in the crowd realize that I'm not "popping" and "locking," I'm rigidly moving only my fingers, "copying" and "pasting" (special—transpose—values).

Next, I imagine myself a wealthy old man and circle a halo over my head with one hand. I'm the Angel Investor, and I pretend to flick money out of my pocket, as if I'm willing to offer start-up capital to businesses on generous terms. I'm feeling particularly generous, and I flick out real currency to a few excited onlookers.

The Excel Modeler

A few minutes into the session, a different girl tugs at me in an effort to pull me out of the circle, and I stop to catch my breath and chat with her for a second. We go through the familiar pleasantries, and as she fidgets with an earring, she tells me that she's a Retail Banker at Wachovia.

Ouch, I think, the corners of my mouth pulling back in embarrassment for her. I know what I have to do; it's mean, but it has to happen. Rule #2. Taking a step away, I wave one finger in front of her face. The No Interest Loan lets her know that, like the name of the dance move, she doesn't exist.

Hurt splatters across her face, and I feel a moment of remorse. Perhaps that was too harsh. It's obvious that she just wants to be included, so out of pity, I lead her to dance on a table and encourage her to begin the Asset Stripper. "Pour Some Sugar on Me!" she sings along, gyrating like a sorority girl after too many games of flip cup, and we value her like a company, deciding which parts we'd keep or sell off.

"Kinda nice cheekbones!" Jon screams. "Her ankles aren't bad either," I add. We put our fingers to our lips and humor her for a second, but ultimately, we decide she's a bad opportunity and move on.

In search of lubrication, I head over to the bar to order three shots of Jägermeister. The bartender doesn't even have to ask me what I'm ordering; she just knows and doles out the viscous black Banker grease.

As I'm returning, I hear the horrific thumping of that *Knight Rider* Panjabi MC song. "Noo!" I scream at the DJ. "Fuck you!" The entire club turns and focuses on Gopal, as if he's meant to instruct them on how to properly move to the music. "It's your song!" someone screams and points. He blushes, loving his one moment in the limelight.

I lazily down my Jäger and watch Gopal's two seconds of fame. He's on a roadshow, raising capital left and right—I'm pleased with how his IBD-envy is manifesting itself. But just

then, Gopal begins to modify the dance, en-
acting an odd, screwing-in-lightbulbs
variation.

What the hell is that? I think,
watching his shoulders move up and
down rapidly, as if possessed. After a moment, I deduce that it's something sort
of *ethnic.*

Infuriated, I get his attention and
hold three fingers in front of my
face. "Rule number three," I mouth, turning
my hand around in emphasis. Realizing
he's violated the code, he returns to
our better, more Banker, and more
American routine.

Raise the Capital

I shake off that experience and start heading back toward
the dance area, but I'm quickly distracted. I spot a beautiful,
blond debutante swaggering through the club. This girl, however, is in a *black* sundress, and she's overloaded with self-
confidence. As she approaches, I act totally blasé and press
my phone to my ear, putting one finger to my lips. I mouth
"On a Call" to her as she passes and shake my head, uninter-
ested. She's confused at first, but stops and considers the situation. The move never fails, and like the people near my desk
at work, she shuts up and lets me get down to business.

Her name is Emily, and it becomes immediately apparent
that this is the kind of girl who methodically hunts prestige

in men, following the league tables just so she will know who to sleep with. Unabashed, she asks, "So, what do you do in The City?"

Innovative question, I admit to myself. I start to respond, but halt as I hear that the DJ has recalibrated. He puts on "Raise Up" by Petey Pablo, and I decide. I'll *show* rather than *tell* her with the Private Chopper. The Wachovia girl screeches in glee from across the bar, pleased by the reference to her company's headquarters in North Carolina. But there's still no interest in her.

On a Call

In a swift movement, I remove my building badge and whip it around my head like a helicopter.*

With the eyes of an intrigued child, Emily looks up at the plastic card. Eager to know what it says, she nearly jumps off her toes to grasp it. At last, she catches the name of my Bank in the strobe light, and awe spreads over her face. I hear her gasp, and her lip nearly bleeds, she bites it so hard.

My badge is like a Banker version of the bat signal, and Emily's friend comes running over to join. "I'm Ashley," she offers eagerly, bouncing and waving.

"Oh I know," I respond, instinctively. Then I add: "I work on the *Buy* Side."

The three of us dance together in a little Double Gearing. Sandwiched between them, mashing up and down to "Igni-

---

*This move can't be implemented by those who work at shitty Banks.

tion," I'm a Bank working with multiple insurance companies, except I'm not that kind of Bank, and insurance companies are, in general, disgusting.

The clinic continues to the tunes of Destiny's Child, Big Pun, Blackstreet, and Prince. "Sweet Child o' Mine" gets bookended by "Come on Eileen" and Paula Abdul's "Straight Up." When "Song of the South" comes on, I almost go hoarse screaming: "This is my JAM!"

$$\$\ \$\ \$$

I sit down with my girls for a while, half-listening as they gossip, each referring to the other by what sounds like a letter, not a first name. Looking out at the dance floor I realize it must

The Private Chopper

be late, as Jon is still out there, now stumbling around drunk doing the Random Walk to "Dancing with Myself." I briefly try to predict the movements of his feet, but it's impossible. I want to find an underlying pattern to Jon's lurching, but Efficient Market Theory also apparently applies to drunk dancing.

The crowd has thinned, and Gopal is in a corner pretending to text someone I know doesn't exist. I send him a quick

SMS, and I see that he reads it immediately. He turns back to me, wounded, and, to emphasize his failure, I mouth the text to him, slowly: "GOOD LUCK IN THE SPRRRING, FITZWATER."

With Gopal now in tears, it's time for me to exit gracefully, so I grab my two conquests by the hand and start to leave the club with them in tow.

On my way out, I pass the DJ. I look at him curiously, still trying to figure out how he managed to pack so many hit Banker tracks onto his laptop. He throws up a strong fist as I walk by, and on his finger, I think I spot a Princeton ring that matches my own.

The sight of the Shield takes me back, and I realize that since school, these past couple years have gone exactly as planned. I'm a young, successful financier in New York with more money than I can spend. I work in The Greatest Profession on Earth. I'm wearing four-hundred-dollar loafers and a custom-tailored shirt I might just throw away because it's got a spot of Jäger on it. I actually took a night away from getting bottles, only to end up going home with two drop-dead gorgeous girls who insist on calling each other "Em" and "A."

Damn, it feels good to be a Banker.

I continue walking, and the bouncer opens the door in grand fashion for me and my girls. Exiting, I free one hand and bang an imaginary bell over my head. The market is closed.

PERFORMANCE REVIEW #4

1. There is a thirty-second line outside of a club, and there is an open bar all night. Bottle service costs $400 for two bottles. What is the most appropriate way to roll?

   The correct answer: buy bottles.

2. Rate the following artists on a scale of 1 (hipster) to 10 (Banker):
   - a. Death Cab for Cutie
   - b. John Mellencamp
   - c. Michelle Branch
   - d. Green Day
   - e. Creed

   The correct answer: a,e,d,c,b.

3. Is X a Banker song?

   1. X is from the eighties.

   2. X is by Madonna.

      a. Statement (1) by itself is sufficient to answer the question, but statement (2) by itself is not;

      b. Statement (2) by itself is sufficient to answer the question, but statement (1) by itself is not;

      c. Statements (1) and (2) taken together are sufficient

to answer the question, even though neither statement by itself is sufficient;

d. Either statement by itself is sufficient to answer the question;

e. Statements (1) and (2) taken together are not sufficient to answer the question, requiring more data pertaining to the problem.

The correct answer: d.

4. You work at Bank of America. Which of the following dances are you *not* permitted to do?

a. The Private Chopper

b. The Top Tier

c. The Random Walk

d. All of the above

The correct answer: d.

5. Benefits are ways for Bankers to

a. Rationalize an open bar

b. Dance to live music

c. Save lives

d. Blow money on auctions

e. All of the above

The correct answer: c.

6. If you are a Banker, you are living the _____.

Conclusion

I CAN ONLY IMAGINE that the majority of the material in this book went over your head. Nonetheless, I hope that reading these facts and stories from my prestigious life and my burgeoning career in finance has left you with an inexplicable sense of something in the base of your stomach. That feeling is envy.

You should now, at the very least, have a better understanding of society's most elite subset. I'm only beginning my personal journey on Wall Street and will be tearing it up for a long time to come. So if you do find yourself among Bankers for some reason, it's not necessary to flex your newfound knowledge or try to relate to us. No—just show some deference and get the hell out of our way.

I'm not going to thank you for reading this text, as it was I who did you a service. Nonetheless, I'll leave you with a ritual compliment Bankers pay to one another after times of great accomplishment and significant global impact.

"Good work this week."

Acknowledgments

I'd like to thank the following institutions
for their commitment to serving Bankers:

Tenjune
John Allen
Hampton Jitney
Hermès Shop Girls
Lord Willy's
Research In Motion
Wilhelmina Models
Bonobos Pants
The Patriot Saloon
Q
Teterboro Airport
Bergdorf Goodman
917-988-0069 (beeper)
The Microsoft Office Suite

Also: my agent, Byrd—you would have made an excellent Trader. My editor, Brendan—strong attention to detail. And Amit Chatwani, the Indian drone to whom I outsourced the actual typing of this text. Any errors are due to his lack of fluency.